Issues in Medical Research Ethics

Teaching Ethics: Material for Practitioner Education (TEMPE)

General Editor: Donna Dickenson, John Ferguson Professor at the University of Birmingham and Director of the Centre for the Study of Global Ethics

These three books introduce key areas in current medical ethics to readers with no previous knowledge in the field. Structured around a variety of guided activities and real-life cases, the books look respectively at the implications of the possible abuses of new reproductive technologies, "new genetics", and protection of research subjects in an increasingly global environment of research trials. Both authors and cases represent a wide range of European backgrounds and professional disciplines, including medicine, bioethics, law, sociology, theology, and philosophy. A video further enhances the value of these workbooks.

Volume 1

Ethics of New Reproductive Technologies: Cases and Questions

Dolores Dooley, Joan McCarthy, Tina Garanis-Papadatos, Panagiota Dalla-Vorgia +

Volume 2

Ethics and Genetics: A Workbook for Practitioners and Students

Guido de Wert, Ruud ter Meulen, Roberto Mordacci, Mariachiara Tallacchini

Volume 3

Issues in Medical Research Ethics

Jürgen Boomgaarden, Pekka Louhiala, Urban Wiesing

Issues in Medical Research Ethics

Edited by

Jürgen Boomgaarden
Pekka Louhiala
Urban Wiesing

Berghahn Books
New York • Oxford

First published in 2003 by **Berghahn Books**
www.BerghahnBooks.com

Library of Congress Cataloging-in-Publication Data

Issues in medical research ethics / edited by Jürgen Boomgaarden,
Pekka Louhiala, Urban Wiesing.
p.cm -- (Teaching Ethics: Material for Practitioner Education; vol.3)
Includes bibliographical references and index.
ISBN 1-57181-601-1 (hardback : alk. paper)
1. Medicine--Research--Moral and ethical aspects. 2. Medical
sciences--Research--Moral and ethical aspects. 3. Medical ethics.
I. Boomgaarden, Jürgen. II. Louhiala, Pekka. III. Wiesing, Urban.

R724 .I83 2003
174'.28--dc21

British Library Cataloguing in Publication Data

A catalogue record for this book is available from the British Library
Printed in the United States on acid-free paper

ISBN 1-57181-601-1 hardback

Contents

Contributors

Richard Ashcroft

Jürgen Boomgaarden

Donna Dickenson

Melanie Jones

Salla Lötjönen

Pekka Louhiala

Giovanni Maio

Georg Marckmann

Juan Viñas-Salas

Paul Wainwright

Urban Wiesing

Introduction

TEMPE (Teaching Ethics: Material for Practitioner Education) is a two-year research project (2000–2002) funded by the European Commission Framework-5 Programme. The title itself was chosen to encompass the research, workshops and production of texts, a CD-ROM and a video all carried out with the intent to explore three major themes: ethics in new reproductive technologies, in medical research itself and in genetics. The chief coordinator of TEMPE is Donna Dickenson, formerly of Imperial College School of Medicine, London, and currently professor at the Centre for Global Ethics, University of Birmingham. Professor Dickenson's experience with a previous open-learning BIOMED-2 project proved invaluable in advising the process of developing TEMPE. Researchers associated with the project come from a variety of disciplines and are affiliated with universities in Greece, Ireland, Germany, Finland, Italy, the Netherlands and the United Kingdom. The project focuses on the development of a set of workbooks, which are open-ended in their intent to provoke thoughtful analysis within the scope of the three core themes in health care ethics, and which are to be made available on a European-wide basis.

Issues in medical research ethics is the result of the partnership between Imperial College, the University of Helsinki and the University of Tübingen.

The authors of this text wish to acknowledge the contribution of all participants of the workshops in medical research ethics held in Tübingen, Germany (July 2000), and in Hämeenlinna, Finland (September 2000), as well as the contribution of the participants in the users' workshop in Tübingen (June 2001). Those who have contributed specific cases, commentaries on cases or articles are acknowledged in the text itself and in the references. A complete list of all participants in the three workshops appears at the end of the workbook.

The authors also wish to acknowledge the comments of the critical readers of the first draft of the workbook. A full list of the critical readers appears at the end of this workbook.

Issues in medical research ethics reflects the issues and concerns confronted in clinical practice throughout Europe today, and presents varying national responses in law and policy to these concerns, as identified by ethicists, lawyers, theologians and practitioners who prepared the papers from which the workbook was created. The papers and case studies appear with a varying degree of detail: some are presented in their entirety, with a reading guide and activities included to help the reader assimilate the information discussed into his or her own practice environment; some are presented in excerpted form, allowing a wider range of contributions to be represented.

Chapter one, *On the nature of research*, begins with an advertisement with which patients are recruited for a clinical trial. The wording of the advertisement will raise critical concerns leading to a fundamental question about the nature of research; namely, what differentiates scientific research from clinical practice? By attempting to answer this question, we confront the special ethical problems particular to scientific research as opposed to clinical practice.

The second chapter, entitled *Regulation of research*, begins with a case which explores the questions pertaining to a subject's rights and, thereby, considers especially the claims of ownership of research samples. After critically examining this issue, we will discuss a further critical point with regard to the regulation of research: the inducement to participate in research. This theme is to be illuminated from two different ethical standpoints: from a more libertarian standpoint and from that based on the idea of dignity.

The third chapter, *Research versus consent*, further demonstrates the importance of informed consent. The first case describes taking saliva samples from drug addicts, who, understandably, are very unwilling to give written permission. After a critical commentary is presented, the question of paternalism, of whether and how much paternalism can be recommended, is discussed. Then we examine the ethical issues surrounding the use of women as subjects in clinical research. Finally, a further paper considers the difficult question of the ethical responsibility necessary for research in emergency settings.

Vulnerable groups, the fourth chapter, opens with a case about 'challenging behaviour'. People with learning disability sometimes display what is known as challenging behaviour, which is understood as culturally abnormal behaviour of such intensity that a person is likely to place him or herself in serious jeopardy. A trial is proposed to determine whether the use of a particular antipsychotic medication is effective for managing challenging behaviour. Here a host of ethical problems arise, concerning issues of consent, research on psychiatric patients and the like. A further paper presents fundamental philosophical deliberations: To what extent can research on decisionally-impaired persons be ethically justified at all? Finally, a case is presented concerning the open trial of a drug for Alzheimer's disease.

In the concluding chapter, *The extent of the researcher's duties*, the focus of the work presented is on the role of the sponsor or of the scientific community in the course of research, and which duties a researcher should assume in regard to them. The first case concerns an investigational drug, which has been used to treat patients who have previously been involved in phase III randomised double-blind placebo controlled trial and are about to convert to an open label extension study.

The chapter concludes with remarks on to what extent poorly planned or sloppily performed research represents an ethical problem. This again addresses the initial question of the aims of research and those of medical practice.

This book has been designed to help you, the reader, familiarise yourself with the ethical problems of medical research involving human subjects, and to assist you in making your own decisions by presenting here the most important arguments pertaining to this topic in the field of medical ethics.

This book offers the following concrete assistance:

1) understanding the basic ethical problems of medical research in its relationship to medical practice (see chapter 1);
2) becoming able to evaluate ethically the elementary regulations of medical research (see chapter 2);
3) learning the special problem of informed consent in medical research in its various aspects (see chapters 3 and 4);

4) identifying and evaluating the ethical problems of medical research with respect to the sponsor or the scientific community (see chapter 5).

After completing this workbook you should be able to do the following:

- distinguish between the internal and external aims in scientific research and medical practice and identify the conflicts between them
- analyse the ethical problem of ownership of human tissues
- describe the idea of moral vulnerability and contrast it with economic vulnerability
- describe the idea of human dignity and its relevance to the protection of the human body
- identify ethical problems in conducting a research study with fringe groups
- outline arguments for and against a weak form of paternalism
- summarise the ethical relevance of the Declaration of Helsinki and the European Convention on Human Rights and Biomedicine for research in emergency settings
- analyse the ethical problems in research on patients where the capability to provide consent is diminished
- outline arguments for and against research with cognitively impaired persons
- analyse the ethical problems in research where the treatment is not essentially new but unevaluated
- identify ethical aspects in international studies
- identify vulnerable groups in human research, especially ethical issues with regard to risk of reproductive toxicity
- state some of the ways in which bad science becomes an ethical problem

We wish you a successful learning experience and much pleasure in working with this book!

– 1 –

On the nature of research

The case of recruiting patients

Case by Pekka Louhiala; commentary by Pekka Louhiala and Urban Wiesing

To advance an initial understanding of the ethical problems confronted while conducting research with human beings, we begin with an advertisement that could be found anywhere in the modern industrial world. A physician, Dr X, from the University Hospital Y, is looking for patients for a clinical trial.

DO YOU SUFFER FROM ANXIETY?

Have you been anxious or worried for over six months without a real and obvious reason? Are you otherwise healthy and not on medication?

Participants sought for drug research!

A clinical study is to be conducted in Finland, in which a new kind of drug will be tested for generalised anxiety disorder. The drugs and visits to research physicians are free for research subjects. Earlier research has shown that the drugs are safe.

You can participate if:

- You are 18 years or older
- You suffer from, for example, restlessness, tremor, muscular tension, breathlessness, palpitations, sweating, nervousness, difficulties in concentration, difficulties in falling asleep

- You do not suffer from any other diseases or mental health disorders
- You are not pregnant or breast-feeding
- You do not abuse alcohol or drugs

You have the chance to get the latest and effective drug for generalised anxiety disorder!

The coordinator of the study is Dr X in University Hospital Y.

If you are interested in participating, please call on weekdays between 10–14: *******

Activity:

What could be problematic with this advertisement?

At first glance this advertisement does not appear very suspect. A closer look, however, reveals several issues that are worth considering. After analysing the text of the advertisement, we will be confronted by some basic moral problems implicit in the research, one of which is the role of the researcher-physician.

The advertisement gives the main information about the project but does not give all the information that should be given. First, the funding of the research is left unclear. If the university has a major role in this project, then the formulation is correct, but if not, then the wording 'Dr X in University Hospital Y' is misleading, although factually correct. Interested potential participants should know whether or not this trial is sponsored and, therefore, possibly influenced by commercial interests.

Second, the advertisement does not mention whether this is a placebo-controlled study. The general ethical issue is whether the use of placebos is justified. In this case the obvious aim of the advertisement is to find participants meeting the criteria for generalised anxiety disorder (GAD), for which there is no generally accepted standard treatment. Thus, the use of placebos is, in principle, justified. However, it should be clearly stated in the advertisement that half of the study subjects will be receiving placebos.

Third, the wording leaves unclear whether everyone fulfilling the criteria will be included in the study. On a superficial reading one might think so. It is, in fact, probable that a *majority* of those making initial contact with the researchers will not be included in the study since they do not meet the criteria for GAD.

Medicalisation

The advertisement does not clearly separate symptoms occurring in everyday life from diseases that should be treated. Do not we all sometimes suffer from the 'symptoms' listed? Why should they be 'treated' medically? In general, do not we often have problems pertaining to the struggles of daily life that are not medical problems?

The advertisement opens with a question: 'Have you been anxious or worried for over six months …' However, under the conditions for participation, the advertisement lists symptoms that nearly everyone suffers from without mentioning the period of time of that suffering, as is the case in the first sentence. One of the conditions is described as follows: 'You do not suffer from any other diseases or mental health disorders.' This could be interpreted as meaning the reader began having symptoms over six months ago, though a few sentences later only 'symptoms' are mentioned, and then the advertisement speaks of 'other diseases'. This can be interpreted as indicating that everyone with the symptoms mentioned is suffering from a disease. However, almost all human beings suffer from some of these symptoms at any particular time—and are not suffering from a disease. Therefore, the wording of the advertisement could cause people to believe that the symptoms listed constitute a disease: healthy individuals become patients, and varieties of 'normal' human experience become a disease. The advertisement insinuates that the potential participant is suffering from at least one disease, and that he or she is in need of therapy. It encourages the medicalisation of life, i.e., describing more and more phenomena of life in medical terms.

For us, medicalisation of life is a phenomenon that should be avoided. However, the unwanted side effect of this kind of advertising should be weighed against other possible effects.

The wording may be a means of finding people living with GAD who have never previously thought that they could be helped. If such people are found and if they are helped, either by the medication or by other therapeutic means suggested by the research personnel, this advertisement will have done some good as well.

Activity:

How could you weigh the good done to people who might be helped by the experiment against the harm inflicted on people who become more anxious when they in fact have no disorder?

Is the drug 'effective' or not?

A further and more critical problem arising from the wording of the advertisement is that it presents two contradictory messages. On one hand, it states that 'a new kind of drug is tested for generalised anxiety disorder', but on the other hand, it continues that there is 'the chance to get the latest and effective drug for generalised anxiety disorder'. If the second statement is true, the first sentence is wrong. If the drug is 'effective' there is no need for this trial. One of the two sentences must be wrong.

The contradictory statements present us with a typical problem of clinical research: One cannot promise research subjects that the drug being tested is safe and effective (as there would be no need for a trial if this were so). Research always carries with it a certain risk to the patient or participant involved. The question that should then be asked is whether physicians are allowed to expose patients to certain risks in order to advance science? This leads us to the need to clarify the different roles of physician and researcher, and to analyse the basic problems of research.

The role of the researcher can be clarified by considerations relating to the nature of scientific research; the role of the physician by considerations relating to the nature of medical practice. In the following section, G. Marckmann describes the aims of scientific research, then the aims of medical practice, and finally considers their relationship to one another and the basic conflict between them both.

The conceptual foundations of scientific research and medical practice

by Georg Marckmann[1]

Introduction

Understanding the conceptual foundations of scientific research and medical practice will help to identify and clarify ethical conflicts arising in biomedical research, especially for physicians who engage in scientific inquiry. In this paper I will try to explore the conceptual relationship between scientific research and medical practice: Are they both an integral part of medicine or rather two separate, if not opposing endeavours? I will argue that scientific research and medical practice are two distinct human activities, each defined by its specific *internal aims*. Accordingly, different basic norms guide scientific research and medical practice and lie at the heart of many ethical dilemmas that physicians encounter if they conduct research on human subjects in the search for generalised knowledge.

It seems useful to begin with a definition of science and medicine to determine the conceptual relationship between both disciplines. However, this turns out to be a rather difficult task, as both medicine and science are methodologically diverse disciplines. By defining their internal or intrinsic aims, I will try to elaborate the characteristic features of medical practice and scientific research.

The aims of scientific research

In general, science can be defined in (at least) three different ways: 1) as a *human activity* characterised by certain aims (scientific *research*), 2) as a *social subsystem* (comprising the institutions and individuals involved in scientific research) and 3) as a *body of knowledge*. In order to compare medical practice and scientific research, I will focus on the first aspect

1 This paper derives partly from my article 'Teaching science vs. the apprentice model–do we really have the choice?' *Medicine, Health Care and Philosophy* 4: 85–89. 2001.

and define science in reference to its *internal aim* that guides and determines scientific inquiry. Accordingly, science can be defined as the *methodological and systematic acquisition of generalisable knowledge* through careful investigation, conducting observational or experimental studies and formulating hypotheses, models and theories. Whereas this internal aim, the systematic acquisition of knowledge, represents the defining feature of scientific inquiry, science can serve several external goals and purposes. These *external aims* of science include not only the personal aims of the scientists, who seek recognition, money or academic reward, but also social goals such as increasing general prosperity, enhancing our ability to treat diseases, providing faster and more economical means of transportation or improving our communication system. The distinction between the internal and external aims of science can already be helpful in framing ethical conflicts in biomedical research. There is, for example, the case of scientific misconduct, in which an investigator violates the standards of methodologically sound research (that are implied by the internal aim of scientific research) in order to accelerate his or her academic career (which constitutes an external aim). Another example would be conflicts of interests that can occur if investigators who test the efficacy and safety of a new drug (internal aim) are shareholders in the drug-producing pharmaceutical company (external aim).

Activity:

Fill in the small tabular chart. Enter into the first column the internal aim that is mentioned in the text; and then enter the external aims into the second column. Add additional aims as you find appropriate.

	Internal aims	External aims
Scientific research		
Medical practice		

The aims of medical practice

Let us now proceed with an analysis of the conceptual foundations of medicine. First of all, medicine is a very heterogeneous discipline, which might be one of the main reasons that medicine has so persistently defied a simple classification. Physicians rely on different kinds of scientific and nonscientific knowledge for diagnosis and treatment, they use a wide variety of strategies in clinical decision making, and they practice in quite different settings. Some physicians also engage in experimental research or clinical trials. It is this methodological diversity that makes it so difficult to develop a comprehensive definition of medicine. For the purpose of this paper, I will therefore limit my inquiry to the question: Is there a unique feature that distinguishes medicine from other human activities? Along with other authors (Wieland 1975, Munson 1981, Wiesing 1993, Pellegrino 1999), I would like to argue that the basic, defining feature of the different forms of medical practice is the *internal aim* of medicine: *the promotion of health by the prevention or treatment of disease*. It is the central task of medicine to help the sick cope with their disorders of health. These intrinsic aims make medicine a distinctive kind of human activity, as a response to the universal human experience of illness. The internal aims of medicine determine not only the technical practice of medicine but also the moral obligations and principles that govern medical practice.

As with science, medicine also serves *external aims*. These goals are socially constructed and show considerable variation over time and across different cultures. While these external aims can be identical with the internal aims of medicine (the promotion of health), they also 'open medicine to possible subversion by economics, politics, social ideology, or government and this openness is an ever present threat to the integrity of medicine as practice' (Pellegrino 1999: 60). Yet, the rapid scientific and technological progress in biomedicine, an ageing population and ever-rising health care costs may require a reexamination of the traditional (external) goals of medicine.

Activity:

Supplement the table illustrated above with the designated main internal aim of medicine, but consider that here the external aim may be identical with the internal aim.

In the following section, it will be demonstrated that the internal aims of scientific research and medical practice can compete with each other.

The relationship between scientific research and medical practice

Whereas medicine and science do not necessarily differ in their external aims (for example, both can aim at improving the general prosperity of society), there is a fundamental difference between medicine and science with respect to their *internal aims*. Science aims at furthering our generalisable knowledge while medicine aims at relieving the pain and suffering of sick individuals. While this discrepancy justifies the claim that medicine should not be regarded as a science, it does not imply that medicine is unscientific. On the contrary, medicine can be scientific in as much as it is based on the prudent application of scientific knowledge. Yet it would be a problematic means-to-an-end argument to infer from the fact that medicine employs scientific concepts and theories that medicine is, therefore, a science. Scientific knowledge is not the aim of medical practice, but rather a *means* to perform effectively medicine's central task of promoting or restoring health.

The different internal aims of medical practice and scientific research generate potentially conflicting obligations for physicians who engage in clinical research. As *healer*, the physician's primary obligation is his or her patient's welfare. Based on the best available knowledge and his or her personal skills, the physician has got to choose the most effective therapy that best promotes the patient's well-being and minimises the risk of harm for the patient. As *researcher*, the physician is obligated to perform methodologically sound investigations to advance the body of generalisable and validated knowledge in the domains of medicine and health care. Knowledge about the efficacy and safety of new therapeutic regimes, however, can only be advanced by conducting studies with human subjects. Randomised controlled trials, the gold standard of clinical investigation, require the enrolment of large groups of patients and the randomised assignment of patients to different treatment regiments. The compliance with the study protocol can limit the physician's flexibility to tailor the treatment to the individual needs and values of his or her patients, hence creating a conflict with the physician's obligation to provide for them the best available treatment. Unlike medical practice, which aims at helping individual patients, scientific research disregards the individuality of each patient in order to gain generalisable knowledge about different classes of patients.

Activity:

Marckmann's argumentation is built upon the difference he qualifies between internal and external aims. This distinction is controversial. Is it a difference presented as a statement of fact or postulated as a tool for analysis?

Consider once again the features of the controversial distinction examined here:

- The internal aim of medicine is defined as a distinctive kind of human activity, as a response to the universal human experience of illness.
- In opposition to this, the external aims are socially constructed and show considerable variation through time and in different cultures.

Does this imply that the internal aim of medicine is a more 'natural' activity of the human being and that the external aims are more understood as cultural activities? Is this convincing?

The irresolvable ethical dilemma of clinical research

These conflicting obligations pose an irresolvable ethical dilemma for the physician as healer and researcher, which Richard Toellner has called the 'ethical aporia' of modern medicine (Toellner 1990). The physician has the obligation to treat the patient based on *scientific knowledge*, which is nowadays the best available knowledge and the most powerful means to perform the task of medicine. The scientific validation of medical knowledge, however, requires the exposure of human subjects to the risk of new therapeutic regimes and therefore conflicts with the physician's obligation to, above all, prevent harm (*primum nil nocere*). In other words, it is unethical to use a therapy that has not been validated by scientific investigation; but it is also unethical to assess the efficacy and safety of a therapy through scientific investigation. The basic norms of medical practice and scientific inquiry are either mutually exclusive or mutually restrictive (cf. Toellner 1990: 8).

This fundamental conflict of obligation cannot be resolved unless we completely abandon clinical research. As we would lose our most powerful instrument for performing the practice of medicine, there is a wide consensus that experiments with human subjects in clinical studies are generally justified. Therefore, we can only try to *regulate* the conflict between medical practice and scientific research by establishing *ethical guidelines* (as in the World Medical Association Declaration of Helsinki → Appendix 3, p.123) and *formal procedures* to ensure the compliance with these ethical guidelines (as with institutional review boards, IRBs). However, it is important to realise that even the most thoughtful and conscientious review of a duly constituted IRB will not be able to resolve the underlying ethical predicament of clinical research.

Activity:

Marckmann has concentrated on the ethical dilemma between medical practice and scientific research, which is personified in the physician as healer and researcher. This demonstrates a problem that we will repeatedly encounter in the following articles. Try to draw up a case where you think that the conflict between medical practice and scientific research is so great that scientific research should not be allowed!

– 2 –

Regulation of research

In the first chapter we have become familiar with the most basic problems of medical research involving human subjects. The confusing formulation of the advertisement led us to basic considerations of the relationship between scientific research and medical practice. One conclusion we drew was that the conflict between medical practice and scientific research can be regulated, but not completely resolved.

In all subsequent chapters, ethical problems involving certain forms of regulation of research will be discussed. In particular, the special dilemmas surrounding the issue of informed consent will be examined. In addition, further external forms of regulation of medical research and the associated ethical problems will be discussed. For example, the question of ownership of research samples and the question of inducement when recruiting subjects are covered in this chapter. The following fictive case will address the question of ownership of research samples.

The Case of DNA samples

Modelled after a case study by Ruth Chadwick[2]

Scenario One

A pharmaceutical company is conducting a randomised controlled trial to test the safety and efficacy of a new drug

---

2 Chadwick, R. 2000. Informed Consent in genetic research. In: Doyal, L. and J. Tobias (eds). *Informed Consent in Medical Research*, pp. 203–10. London: BMJBooks.

for a chronic disease. As part of the protocol the pharmaceutical company proposes to collect DNA samples from the population of research subjects receiving the new drug (all of whom suffer from the chronic disease) to establish whether there is any relationship between genetic make-up of the subjects and their response to the new drug in terms of either recovery or side effects. The subjects will be asked to give separate consent to taking part in the trial of the drug, on the one hand, and to the genetic aspects of the trial, on the other.

Scenario Two

The pharmaceutical company proposes to keep some samples from the trial in Scenario One in order to do research on other genetic markers and the possible links between these markers and conditions other than those associated with the chronic disease. In this case, those who agree to participate will have their samples stored after the end of the clinical trial in a DNA bank for research on an unspecified range of conditions. The subjects who participate in the aspect of the trial to test the new drug for the chronic disease will be asked to give a separate consent to the use of their samples to do research on other genetic markers.

Scenario Three

Subjects Smith and Jones, who suffer from the chronic disease, agree to participate in the trial of the new treatment. They also agree to participate in the genetic research linking their response with genetic predispositions, and agree to their samples being put in a DNA bank for further as yet unspecified genetic research. Unfortunately, the new drug does not help Smith and Jones. During the genetic research on their samples, however, it is found that they both share a particular genetic characteristic that leads to the highly effective treatment of another severe disease. The pharmaceutical company markets a 'wonder drug' for this severe disease and makes a substantial profit. Smith and Jones are not entitled to any share in these profits because they signed a consent form acknowledging that they had no right to any commercial benefits arising from the research.

Activity:

Try to imagine yourself in the situation of Smith and Jones. How would you feel? Would you feel that you had been treated improperly? Where do you think the case of injustice could be made in the above scenario? Do you think this injustice could be justified as proper or necessary?

In the following commentary D. Dickenson examines the so-called Moore decision, an actual legal precedent, after which the fictional case described above is patterned. One of the main problems of the fictional case is whether Smith and Jones have any rightful claim to their tissue. Dickenson considers this problem as she discusses the issue of the relationship of the individual to his or her body. The author advances the discussion from the level of the individual subject to the public policy level and poses the question of how a property regime could be developed for genetic material extracted from human tissues.

Commentary on the case

by Donna Dickenson

Although this case is fictional, it derives from a very real and troubling legal precedent, the *Moore* decision of 1990. In the course of a splenectomy, it was discovered that Mr Moore's T-cells (which control immune response) were unusually active. He was asked by the clinician and researcher involved, Dr Gold, to return several more times to the hospital in order to 'donate' further tissue samples, including samples of blood, semen and other bodily substances in addition to T-cells. This, he was told, was a necessary part of his follow-up treatment. In fact, the T-cells taken from Mr Moore during the operation and return visits were developed into a $3-billion cell line, whose profits were accrued solely by the University of California at Berkeley (where the hospital was located) and to the research team.

Mr Moore brought a lawsuit against the university to claim that he had not given an informed consent to the further use of his tissue for the development of a cell line, and that he was entitled to a share of the proceeds. The court found in favour of the first claim, but against the second. Although Mr Moore had consented to the splenectomy, it could not be said that he had given a properly informed consent to further tissue extraction, because he had been deliberately deceived. However, the court held that regardless of the shoddy and fraudulent procedure followed by Dr Gold, the researchers and the university hospital were the sole owners of the cell line developed from Mr Moore's T-cells.

Many people find this result surprising, but it is in fact consistent with the general common law principle of *res nullius*: once taken from the body, genetic material or tissue is 'no one's thing'. Before the advance of biotechnology, it was reasonable to assume that no one could have any interest in tissue extracted from the body, since it was likely to be diseased. The patient's only interest lay in recovery from whatever malignant condition was manifested in the tissue, and therefore in the tissue's excision. As we can see in Ruth Chadwick's case, this is no longer a viable proposition. Smith and Jones have an interest in being cured of their chronic disease, but it may also rightly be said that they have an interest in the further use of the genetic material that has been extracted from them in the course of the clinical trial to find a cure for the chronic disease.

Activity:
Compare the Moore case with the fictional one. Aside from the similarities, can you also name ethically relevant differences?

The Moore case illustrates the old legal maxim, 'Hard cases make bad law'. Consent was violated so egregiously that the court, understandably enough, concentrated its attention on righting the wrong that had been done when Mr Moore was lied to and deceived. But in Ruth Chadwick's case, the researchers have not acted fraudulently. In three successive scenarios, they have carefully obtained separate consents which protect them against the sort of action brought by Mr Moore. More relevantly to European practice (*Moore* is a US case, and there are no European counter-examples), the researchers should have followed perhaps procedures such as those recommended by the Nuffield Council in its discussion paper on property in stem cells (2000) and in the fourth draft of the Medical Research Council guidelines, both of which stress the need to obtain a separate consent for the further development of tissue or genetic material, in addition to the original consent for the procedure by which that material was extracted from the research subject or patient. The Nuffield Council guidelines cover exactly the sort of example presented by Chadwick: stem cell lines may well be used by pharmaceutical companies such as the one in the fictional case to test differential, genetically based response patterns to drugs, and indeed this is one of the prime commercial motives for their development.

Yet, it is not necessarily obvious that Smith and Jones have any rightful property in the tissue merely because it was extracted from their bodies. The pharmaceutical company and its researchers would no doubt present the Lockean claim that the profits belong to those who have laboured to create them. We do not actually have a property in our bodies, even if most people think they do own their bodies (Waldron 1988, Dickenson 1997). There is something incoherent and philosophically contradictory about thinking that we do. After all, we are our bodies; how can we conceive of ourselves as a separate entity from them, bodiless subjects who own the bodily object? Even under the European Human Rights legislation, it seems unlikely that any such notion will be sustainable.

So have Smith and Jones just been very unlucky? Both subjects knew when they agreed to take part in the trial of the new drug that it might or might not help their condition; in the end, it did not, but assuming genuine research trial equipoise, neither the subjects nor the researchers knew in advance whether the new drug would be effective, or effective for whom. It is again only a matter of luck (good or bad, depending on how we look at it) that they do not suffer from the other severe disease, for which the successfully marketed 'wonder-drug' *is* effective. A cure for this severe disease, derived from Smith and Jones's genetic material, turns out to be the great El Dorado, but Smith and Jones are not citizens of that fabled realm.

This analysis may hold at the level of the individual subjects Smith and Jones, but it is patently inadequate at the public policy level. The pharmaceutical company and its like hold all the cards: there is no other game in town. If Smith and Jones want to take part in a trial that may help their condition, they must agree to the terms set down by the research trial funders. Those conditions include consenting to have no part in the profits that may result from further developments made of their genetic material. Similarly, the Medical Research Council and Nuffield draft consent forms only include a box where patients tick that they understand they will have no share in the outcome of any further research developments. There is no place to tick, 'I understand that perfectly well; I just do not agree with it'.

Commentaries on the *Moore* case (e.g., Gold 1996) have queried why the court simply assumed that if Moore had no rights to his tissue after it left his body, that tissue was necessarily the unequivocal property of the researchers and hospital. After all, if *res nullius* means what it says, no one automatically owns the tissue: neither the patient nor the researchers. Even if the researchers had put work into it, they would have no more right over the fruits of their labours than I would have if I cultivated a piece of waste ground, in the full knowledge that it did not belong to me. I could hardly be outraged if in the end I did not get to enjoy the literal fruits of my labours.

It is not too late–especially not in Europe, where the *Moore* precedent does not apply–to develop a different property regime for genetic material extracted from human tissue. There is considerable interest in the idea of benefit sharing as a compromise: firms such as the pharmaceutical company in the fictional case would be allowed to set up tissue banks and extract profits, but only on the condition that they return a proportion of the profit to the medical system of the host country. In Europe, where socialised medical systems are more the norm than in the United States, the structures for doing that already exist. There is also a precedent in reaching agreements to provide forms of ongoing, after-trial health care which biotechnology firms and researchers are being urged to reach with developing countries where they want to hold research trials (Nuffield Council, 2000).

Activity:

Do pharmaceutical companies and other funders of research have ongoing responsibilities to research subjects? If so, how extensive are these responsibilities?

Not only in the spectacular case of a $3-billion cell line, but also in an everyday research trial, financial questions can raise ethical problems. It appears self-evident that the subject who submits to a trial must somehow be financially compensated, but on what basis should such remuneration be measured? Should research subjects be paid an appropriate wage, or should they merely receive symbolic financial recognition? Fundamentally, the question raised is whether, and to what extent, financial inducements are ethically defensible. The next two articles in this chapter deal with these issues from a different standpoint. The first article is based on the idea of moral vulnerability; the second on the idea of dignity.

In the next article, R. Ashcroft defines moral vulnerability, and points out that inducement could be considered one way in which people are said to be morally vulnerable. Ashcroft presents the problem in a model, which demonstrates the difficulties arising from the choices available in a trial for a candidate subject to consider. The underlying question is: Are some choices morally impossible to make, or are there moral limits to the choices that we can invite someone to make. Ashcroft discusses different arguments against offering persons the chance to participate in risky nontherapeutic human experiments. Finally, he explores the question of how inducements can be an instrument of exploitation.

Consent, inducement and conflict of interest in medical research and development

by Richard Ashcroft

A cynic is a man who knows the price of everything, and the value of nothing. *(Oscar Wilde)*

... all inherent contradictions of bourgeois society appear extinguished in money relations... and bourgeois democracy even more than bourgeois economists take refuge in this aspect ... in order to construct apologetics for the existing economic relations. *(Karl Marx 1973: 240)*

The idea of moral vulnerability

Typically, research ethics guidelines and researchers aim at excluding a wide range of people from participation on 'medical' grounds, for example, on grounds of drug addiction, mental illness, allergies, recent history of illness, recent blood donation and so on. In part, this is done to exclude people who will be a raised 'background' risk of experiment-related harm because of underlying physical debility. Also, exclusion of subjects with these kinds of conditions is important for the scientific generalisability and integrity of the research. Finally, members of some of these groups will be *morally* as well as or instead of physically or psychologically vulnerable. The idea of moral vulnerability is that someone is morally vulnerable if he or she is at increased risk of doing something contrary to his or her own interests.

Activity:

We are often doing something contrary to our own interests. Under what circumstances could that develop into a moral problem, or in which cases could such a moral dilemma occur?

In this paper, I will discuss one way in which people are held to be morally vulnerable: they can be 'induced' to do things by paying them, and in particular, they can be induced to take part in risky experiments as subjects. What is such 'inducement'? How does it affect the quality of consent? Should it be regulated and, if so, how?

Activity:

Before you read further, consider what forms of inducement are possible. Perhaps you have heard of someone or already personally experienced someone trying to convince you to accept medical treatment or to participate in a medical experiment. What method did the person use? What factors did he or she exploit? Who offered the inducement?

In the following text, Ashcroft presents a model to assess the place of inducements within medical experimentation.

The risk-benefit assessment

A simple way to think about financial (or other) inducements is as follows. Consider two people, a candidate subject (CS) and an experimenter (B). B proposes to CS that CS join B's experiment. How would CS decide? CS would require, firstly, the information he or she needed concerning the risks to be taken and the benefits he or she could expect from participation in B's experiment. Then CS would need to deliberate about whether the balance of risks and benefits was favourable to him or her. A rational CS would only choose to participate if the balance was favourable.

Notice how complicated this simple model really is. CS must make choices which, philosophically speaking, are profoundly problematic. For instance, CS is to compare sets with sets, rather than singular items – a set of risks with a set of benefits. This presumes that the risks can in effect be aggregated, as can the benefits. Moreover, this discussion of risks is very casual, because it covers true risks (harms with a known or knowable definite probability of occurring), uncertainties (harms with probabilities which are unknowable at the time of choice), frank harms (i.e., risks with probability 1, and which involve a determinate setback to CS's well-being), and a whole range of vague harm-like events or experiences (discomfort or inconvenience) which are of uncertain significance. Next, we are to assume that risks are, within the set of risks, comparable with each other, and that the risks and benefits are comparable between sets. That is, can we offset a 1:100,000 risk of death against the vague but present sense of curiosity piqued and satisfied that participation in experimental research provokes in most academically minded people? In addition, we are to compare present or near-at-hand benefits with harms which are both probabilistic and also distributed at varying temporal distances from the present. The classic example is smoking: I trade a high now for an increased risk (but not a certainty) of an unpleasant death at some point in the future. Finally, the expected benefits need not be considered merely for personal reasons: I may participate for the sake of altruism, even at personal cost. Nor need the benefits be 'obvious' – as mentioned above, a sense of curiosity can be as much a motive as financial want or indeed therapeutic need.

Activity:

Ashcroft has named a variety of risks and benefits. List the types mentioned and add other types that occur to you.

Types of risks	Types of benefit

Let us make the 'simple model' simpler still. Assume, for the sake of argument, all the risks are 'true' risks (events with known probability), that all outcomes (positive or negative) will occur in the short-run time period, and that all outcomes can be measured by a numerical quantity, utility, which is subject to the usual rules of arithmetic. Then all that CS (candidate subject) has to do is compute the following sum:

(Benefit to CS)*(Probability of benefit occurring)-(Harm to CS)*(Probability of harm occurring) = Net benefit of E (experiment) to CS

If CS is rational, then CS will choose according to whether the Net benefit of E to CS is greater than (or equal to) the Net benefit of the next best option available to CS in the time period in question. This is in effect the economists' idea of choosing the option that minimises the 'opportunity cost' faced by the chooser.

Note first of all that the Net benefit of E to CS need not be positive. All that is required for CS to enter E, rationally, is for CS's other options to be even worse. Suppose I am very poor, but healthy, and I have no money and no prospect of getting any soon, and I need to feed my family or they will die of malnutrition–and I can sell one of my kidneys to raise money. Then it is conceivable that while I would be worse off for the lack of the kidney, I would be even worse off with the kidney but also a starving family. The critical issues, here as in human experimentation, are whether I should be able to sell my kidney for money (or food or other benefits), and secondly, if sale is permitted, what would be a fair price. In other words, could the value of cash and the value of a kidney be comparable at all; if they are comparable, is there a moral side constraint that makes sale (though conceptually possible) immoral; if there is no such moral constraint, what makes the transaction a fair one.

Activity:

Ashcroft continuos using the example of the kidney seller in the context of medical experiments. An essential point of comparison lies in the relationship between risk and benefit. Before reading further, sum up, in your own words, the risks and benefits that face the kidney seller. Is there a corresponding relationship In a medical experiment? List the similarities and differences.

Similarities and differences between the kidney seller example and the human experimentation situation

There are similarities between the kidney seller example and the human experimentation situation. If we translate the sale of a kidney and paid participation in experimentation into terms relating to risk, the individual is being paid to undergo a small risk of major harm in each case. Indeed the kidney sale risk is more definite: the perioperative risk is definite (if small) and the long-running chance of the only remaining kidney's failure is definite (if small, and subject to time preference discounting). Yet, the human experimentation risks in a study performed on humans in pharmacology are very indefinite; we know neither the probabilities of harm, nor the nature of the harm, nor the time period in which the harm would become manifest. We know something about the kinds of harm that CS may be exposed to, and generally we have some idea about other similar drugs' action and effects, and we know about how this drug behaved in animal experiments. The principal worries would be the occurrence of sudden death or of irreversible disabling illness or injury. Where kidney 'donation' is irreversible (transplant of another's kidney is not equivalent to not losing one's own in the first place), most human experimentation has short-term effects only, but in some cases this is not so, just as in some cases the remaining kidney may later fail. In effect, the human experimentation case creates even more concern than does the sale of kidneys, because of the uncertainty of what is being agreed to by CS.

While CS is the only one who can make this choice, are there moral limits to the choices that we can invite CS to make? Are some choices morally impossible? Or morally corrupting?

Activity:
Clarify your own ethical perspective by considering possible choices CS should not be asked to make.

Are there convincing arguments against the offer of participation in risky nontherapeutic human experimentation?

Consider first the argument that the offer of participation in risky nontherapeutic human experimentation is immoral, whether or not CS could be brought to agree to participate or not. Then there would be a case for preventing such research, by preventing researchers from approaching CS even to ask for his or her consent. It is on this basis that organ sale is banned in most developed countries. Implementing a ban in the case of research would be based on one of the following:

1) all such research poses a wrongful harm (or substantial risk thereof) to CS;
2) CS would be brought to agree to something that was morally corrupting (if not directly harmful);
3) it reflected badly on a society that allowed such activity to take place and revealed that some people were sufficiently desperate or depraved enough to take part in it;
4) this activity did not harm the average individual subject, but placed vulnerable individuals at risk of agreeing to something contrary to their interests.

All of these grounds have been invoked for placing a ban on such research, especially in debates about sex and drugs, but most of them are open to the standard liberal attack on state paternalism (the idea that one might make decisions that one perceives to be in the best interest of others).

Activity:

Consider the different reasons offered by Ashcroft that explain why the offer of participation in risky nontherapeutic human experimentation should be forbidden. Which reasons are more convincing and which are less so? In your opinion, which are the most paternalistic and thereby open to the 'standard liberal attack'?

Next, consider the argument that because money and risk of serious harm are noncomparable, there is no price that could represent a fair trade of risk for acceptance of an inducement. The first point to notice is that, on the contrary, many people do trade money against risk: gambling, air travel, employment in the fire service, all represent just such a choice. There are limits to this. For example, contract killing is illegal (but that is because killing is illegal). Certain things, it is generally agreed, cannot be sold (Dickenson 1997). The scope of this paper restricts exploring these arguments further. But note that people are actually rather good at developing a price for things (if not a 'value'–remember Karl Marx and Oscar Wilde at the beginning of the article). So it is a little bizarre for philosophers to say that something cannot be sold, if, meanwhile, there is a market for that thing that exists outside their study window. What in effect they, the philosophers, want to say is that it should not be sold (which in the case of human experimentation may again come down to legal moralism) or that while the parties involved may think they are engaged in the act of selling and buying, they are, in fact, doing so where no enforceable contract is in operation (as in surrogacy 'contracts', which are in most jurisdictions unenforceable).

The condition of a fair level of inducement

Finally, we should consider the argument that while we may regret that CS agrees to participate in research for financial inducement, and we may disapprove of people who offer CS money to participate in risky research, we have no grounds to ban the practice; however, we do have grounds for preventing the research from taking place unless there is a fair level of inducement.

Activity:

Ashcroft himself put a condition on risky research, arguing that a fair level of inducement must exist. What might be some of the consequences for allowing risky research to take place, so long as subjects are properly paid?

This argument indicates that (at least some) exploitation should be prevented in medical research.

Space here does not permit a detailed discussion of how legislators and regulators should respond to exploitation; suffice it to say that any system to prevent exploitation per se tends to overlook the fact that exploitation is relative to the individual circumstances, so generic policy solutions tend not to 'bite'. Moreover, prevention of price setting by CS may protect CS from setting a price that is too low judged by an objective standard, but could also force CS to select his or her options from a smaller set (because the research option has been deleted). So the wish to protect CS may leave CS worse off, rather than better off. A more effective means of protecting CS may be to raise CS's background circumstances such that participation in such research is no longer the most attractive option. However, clinical researchers would still need to find CSs from somewhere.

The two kinds of vulnerability

What would appear to be wrong with inducements–if in fact anything is–is that they can be an instrument of exploitation of two kinds of vulnerability: economic vulnerability and moral vulnerability. Economic vulnerability–poverty–raises considerably the analytical difficulties in proposing a limit to inducements, since by limiting a local exploitation (inducing the poor to participate in research) we may intensify a global exploitation (the economic inequity which leads people to need to participate in research). The appropriate analytic and practical remedies for this dilemma are not at hand. Moral vulnerability (here, misguidedly or mistakenly acting against our best interests), born in part in our common human psychological disposition to discount our long-run interests in favour of our short-run interests and to discount unknown risks in the light of known risks and benefits, is possibly easier to remedy through the assistance of research ethics committees, patient advocates and well-constructed information sheets. Procedural solutions may well offer satisfactory means for containing the vulnerability of candidate subjects.

Conclusion

The problem with inducements can be summarised as follows. Economic vulnerability per se is not the main issue. It merely defines the social context within which CSs must choose. Rather, moral vulnerability defines the troubling aspects of inducements. It involves a vulnerability that is common to us all to a great or lesser extent. Inducements threaten morally vulnerable people in situations of economic vulnerability by encouraging them to offset vague, uncertain, probabilistic harms against a clear, certain and present cash benefit: this undercuts one's ability to make what the Nuremberg Code (→ Appendix 1, p.108) calls an 'understanding and enlightened decision' (No.1). However, there are two dangers arising from this understanding of vulnerability. The first is to mistake financial inducement for constraint or coercion; the wrong risked is in fact exploitation. The second mistake is to substitute exploitation with paternalism, including the patronising assumption that vulnerable people cannot choose for themselves at all. Just as we presume a subject capable of consenting to medical treatment, and support even the 'vulnerable' subject in making his or her own choices, so too we should presume such a capability as necessary in conditions of moral vulnerability. The aim should be to remove the exploitation, not the choice.

Activity:

Ashcroft discusses central questions with respect to the problem of the morality of inducements.

Can the subject make decisions to participate in medical research that are morally objectionable? Is the participation in risky, nontherapeutic experiments a choice that the potential subject should not be asked to make?

Is there no price that could represent a fair trade of risk for acceptance of an inducement?

Ashcroft discussed these questions on the basis of certain premises. He understands moral vulnerability as the increased risk of doing something contrary to one's own interest.

In the following article, J. Boomgaarden also discusses the matter of inducement, but approaches the problem from entirely different assumptions, especially with regard to the concept of morality.

Boomgaarden describes a fictive case study and considers first the study from the ethical standpoint of radical autonomy. In contrast to this initial consideration, he develops the idea of the uniqueness of each person. He tries to demonstrate how the altruistic intention can be the only basic ethical justification for participating in experiments of use to others. Yet, he argues that it cannot be the task of the physician-researcher to discover the true intention of the potential research subject.

Human dignity in medical research

by Jürgen Boomgaarden

Whatever has a value can be replaced by something else which is *equivalent*; whatever, on the other hand, is above all value, and therefore admits of no equivalent, has a dignity. (*Immanuel Kant 1988: 63–64*)

A case study

Let us consider a fictive case study.

Imagine that a person participates for the first time in a new drug application trial. When questioned about why he decided to participate in the trial, he replies that his primary reason was that it is a good opportunity to earn extra money. Therefore, he is willing to accept possible risks. Nearly everything in life today, he claims, is associated with some sort of risk. The physician-researcher agrees that he is correct; however, before accepting him for the trial, he wishes to impress upon him the specific risks he will be taking. The potential research subject demurs, because he does not actually want to know the risks in detail since they would make him worry too much. 'Close your eyes and full speed ahead!' is his motto. He trusts that the doctor will perform everything properly, and he needs the money and cannot earn it anywhere else so easily.

In most situations, such a frank discussion about the motives of the potential research subject would not occur. However, such a fictive dialogue is useful for the purposes of a discussion on ethics.

The ethical problem

Is there an ethical problem at all? Should we not leave the potential research subject to decide for himself, and allow him to enter the experimental project on whatever grounds he chooses? Should we not respect the potential subject's ability to determine his own interests? At worst, he can only damage himself, and if he decides to do so, so be it! Also, even if the potential subject reveals a problematical motivation for participating in the research project, this alone does not justify preventing him from participation in the trial. It is only crucial that a potential research subject is neither coerced nor talked into participation in the research project. As long as the potential subject is given the right to refuse participation, no ethical considerations need be explored.

The potential research subject presented here is free to refuse participation, although this would mean a loss of income. At the point at which he can sustain himself only by participation in the human experimentation, compulsion exists.

Even if he does not wish to listen carefully to the information about the risks, in order not to unduly disturb himself, his decision to participate is accepted as reasonable. However, instead of informed consent, a mere consent has occurred, so to speak, in which the potential subject is only informed about the risk involved in as much as he wants to be. Such a consent does not imply deception or compulsion, but rather indicates a protection of the interest of the research subject, who does not wish to be disturbed. The autonomy and the interests of the potential research subject are taken absolutely seriously.

Activity:

Form your own opinion about this argument. What is convincing about the claims for radical autonomy? Would you rather combine the principle of autonomy with other ethical principles?

One can, however, consider the dialogue from another ethical perspective, from which a certain ethical problem does in fact arise. The viewpoint can be defended that it is unworthy for a person to participate in research trials solely on financial grounds. A person cannot protect his or her own sense of human dignity while agreeing to such a research trial, without wanting to inform him or herself of the risks entailed beforehand.

To understand this perspective we must begin with a definition of dignity. This term can be found in some of the most prominent medical guidelines, for example, in the Declaration of Helsinki (→ Appendix 3, p.123), which states: 'It is the duty of the physician in medical research to protect the life, health, privacy, and dignity of the human subject' (B.10).

In this article the term 'dignity' is taken to incorporate the following:
a) the idea of the uniqueness of each person and
b) the idea of the unity of a human being and his or her body.

To what extent is human dignity threatened in the fictive case described above?

The unique aspect of the situation is the 'exchange value': in order to earn the money, the research subject makes his own body available. The risk to his body is paid for, but, what is ethically problematical in this? Many occupations are coupled with a risk to one's physical well-being, and we make no objection to these risks or these occupations. For example, the policeman, the deep-sea diver, the construction worker on skyscrapers and the soldier, to name just a few, all accept the life-threatening aspects of their jobs. Why should the 'professional' research subject be prevented from taking serious risks as well?

Activity:

Before you read further, consider if there is a difference between the professions listed above and the 'profession' of a research subject, with respect to risks involved which could be life-threatening.

The particular situation in research trials

In at least two points the research subject's 'profession' differs from other risky professions. Firstly, in the other occupations injury is accidental, whereas bodily injury to the research subject is, though not intentionally inflicted part of the purpose of drug evaluation. The fact that bodily injuries might occur is entirely possible in a new drug application trial. Indeed, such an occurrence might in some sense be valued as a success, because it is useful for the evaluation of the drug. This is especially true for Phase 1 evaluations of experimental drugs, in which the toxic effects are initially tested. The dose is usually increased in small steps, until one finally arrives at a dose which routinely causes acute side effects. Therefore, in research trials, as opposed to other occupations, the (usually temporary) injuries to the human body are regarded as useful. Another example illustrates this point further: One could decide to save costs on the protective uniforms of soldiers or policemen, and to compensate them financially for the risk that occurs from this measure; assuming such compensation would be deemed more economical. Probably most of us would regard the higher risk entailed in such a measure as ethically problematic.

Secondly, the research subject is much more exposed to possible injury than people in other 'risky' professions. The other activities always include a certain degree of individual responsibility during the activity, and thus the professional is able to avoid dangerous situations through his or her behaviour. In a similar manner the subject does carry a high degree of personal responsibility in the proper handling of the sample. The subject should carefully observe the dose, the frequency of administration, etc., and, in case of problems developing, inform the doctor immediately. But during the actual 'activity' (the reaction of his or her body to the experimental drug) the research subject is condemned to inaction.

At this point we are almost in the position to formulate the ethical problem. The critical question is, whether the physical risks and the temporary helplessness of the research subject can be justified by financial reward, as is the case with other risky human activities. With the indirectly intended risks of injury to the human body, the whole person is involved, putting at stake a certain loss of his or her own human dignity. However, is it possible to calculate a person's worth in monetary terms? Each person is unique. A person does not have a certain value; rather, a person is incommensurable, i.e., there is nothing that is comparable to him or her. He or she is irreplaceable. This defines personal dignity. If there was something comparable in value to an individual person, I could calculate that person's appropriate financial value, but this is not the case. Therefore, there is no predetermined upper financial limit which can be charged for the medical treatment of a person. Without doubt, we would find it immoral if a treatment was discontinued simply because the patient was not deemed worthy of the additional financial costs accumulated.

Activity:

Consider: Is this realistic? Or are there certain situations in which one must, in fact, financially appraise the treatment of a person?

Arguing that, for example, the remaining short life expectancy of the patient is still to be estimated with a financial cost of exactly X would certainly be considered unacceptable. A person cannot be valued against money. Therefore, allowing the human body to be used in research trials for a financial remuneration, as could occur with high financial inducements, is ethically problematic.

The difference between therapeutic research and nontherapeutic research

The question of the ethical justification of a research trial refers not only to the role of inducements but also to the different intentions of the experiments.

The situation is different when the patient could benefit from the experiment. In therapeutic research, the intention is primarily to help the patient through the experiment; whereas in nontherapeutic research, the primary intention is to test a drug for its risks and side effects. Of course, in the latter case, one can claim in a broader sense that the intention of the research trial is also to cure disease. But in nontherapeutic research, the possibly injurious, at best complication-free, intervention does not directly benefit the research subject in combating his or her disease. In a therapeutic trial, discovering possible severe side effects is not the primary intention of the experiment; rather, it is to help a particular set of patients or a single patient, who could potentially benefit from the trial. Therefore, therapeutic trials are justifiable.

However, does this mean that if a trial does not benefit the participant, it is ethically objectionable? Here, the essential intention of the affected person is to be considered. If a research subject participates in a trial in order to benefit the treatment of other sick people, then the risks accepted by the subject may not be judged as too high. The research subject's own body would be placed in a broad sense at the disposal of other persons for their benefit, defining the act of engagement in the trial as a personal sacrifice for the sake of others, not as a means for acquiring monetary reward or for aiding scientific research alone. Only in placing the well-being of another person or 'persons' over one's own is an adequate equivalent found for the sacrifice of one's actual health. This would be the only truly worthy ground for which such a research trial should be considered.

Activity:

Is this argument convincing? Or is the motive of helping others already completely corrupted by the failure of many experiments or by the influence and economical interests of pharmaceutical companies?

It is required that a potential research subject who agrees to take part in a trial do so only after understanding completely the risks involved in the trial. If a potential subject refuses further explanation of the risks involved, as occurs in the fictive case described above, then he or she would thus be harming his or her sense of dignity. A willingness to participate in a trial for the benefit of others coupled with the refusal to know all the risks involved in the trial allows for a degree of self-deception to become an integral part of making an altruistic decision, a self-deception which can only be said to jeopardise a person's dignity. Such a person who acts only on the condition of remaining uninformed presupposes that being informed would prevent him or her from taking part in the trial, due to fear of what might happen. This method of decision making demands a desire for ignorance which counters any definition used to describe a dignified approach to life.

For this reason, the requirement of an *informed* consent plays such a central role in international documents written to outline research involving human subjects, e.g., Declaration of Helsinki B.22 (→ Appendix 3, p.123).

Risk and altruistic motivation

The risks involved in the research trial can now be observed. In most research trials, the possible risks can be approximately evaluated prior to the trial. From an ethical perspective, the level of the expected side effects is of significant importance. The greater the risk, the more relevant the question becomes concerning the motivation of the research subject. In the administering of an experimental drug, where at most only slight side effects are expected to occur, no special altruistic motivations on the part of the patient are needed. For example, a research subject who expresses his or her altruistic motivations to the investigator, but who risks nothing more than a slight headache, could appear foolish, in comparison to someone who is willing to take a higher risk. Thus, in instances of relatively harmless experiments, research subjects need not necessarily be very altruistic. Claims of altruism are of no consequence because of the insignificant risk. The student who wishes to earn some money as a research subject in routine, harmless research trials, is not to be regarded as an example of a possible ethical problem.

Activity:

Or can, in fact, an ethical problem arise here? In your opinion, to what extent are such harmless research trials a problem or a potential problem?

Many people will suffer unwelcome feelings as a result of participating in such trials. Participating in a research trial is not the same as going to the sports club; although the risk of injury in the sports club could be much higher. This 'unwelcome feeling' is connected to the peculiar character of these experiments, as described above. With such an experiment, human dignity is an issue even if the risk to the research subject is insignificant.

It is an entirely different matter if the research subject is willing to take a higher risk, and even put his or her own life in danger in order to earn a large amount of money.

When financial remuneration for the participation in a research trial is large enough to be considered solid income, then caution is certainly required. The affected person creates for him or herself an intrinsic commitment to an income and would become, essentially, the source of his or her income. Such a person would be increasingly more willing to assume higher risks–for who can risk a loss of earnings. Of course, the limits of what a professional research subject can do for this income are set by natural boundaries. There are 'wash-out' periods to be observed. Nevertheless there is a danger, which should be ethically considered.

Moreover, if the recruitment potential for research trials consists only of members from a socially weaker group, then the situation becomes more ethically problematic. The better educated and more financially secure members of society do not need to augment their income through risky experiments on their own bodies. It should be remembered that the participation in research trials is not to be valued as equivalent to every other form of 'normal' work. In this respect, the question about the motivation of the potential subject should assume an important position in the framing and practice of research trials.

Activity:

Perhaps you already know many research subjects at your place of employment. From what social group do they come? What factor does their social environment play in their attitude towards research trials?

Should it be the task of the physician-researcher to ask about the potential research subject's attitude? As already mentioned, such a question is superfluous when the risk involved is extremely low. Additionally, the motivation can be determined through other factors. By instituting a low level of payment, the danger of a financial inducement (which can lead to financial dependency) can be avoided. It certainly cannot be the task of the physician-researcher to perform any kind of 'attitude espionage' on a potential research subject, but the researcher can make it clear that being a research subject is not a 'job'. Thus, the investigator can establish a basis of trust, which is necessary for the performance of most research trials. The physician-researcher depends on his or her subjects to independently observe certain restrictions placed on the subject during the time frame of an experiment (for example, demanding that no additional medications be taken, etc.).

Activity:

On the basis of an imaginary, but standard case, the author considered the role of inducements in medical research. The central idea in this section was the significance of human dignity, which essentially is defined as the uniqueness of each person.

Similar questions were treated differently in the previous articles:

Do you think that the research subject can make morally objectionable decisions regarding his or her participation in medical research? Is, for example, the participation in risky, nontherapeutic experiments reprehensible?

Try to answer the questions for both articles.

In J. Boomgaarden's Kantian-influenced concept, the intention of the researcher not to harm the dignity of the subject could restrict the research subject's choice. Is that morally right?

In R. Ashcroft's utilitarian-influenced concept, the choices allowed the research subject should not be restricted. But is that possible without the danger of exploitation occurring?

– 3 –

Research versus consent

In the previous chapter, fundamental questions on the regulation of research on human beings were considered with respect to their ethical relevance. In particular, the issues of ownership of research samples and of inducement or financial compensation were addressed.

However, in all of these questions pertaining to regulation, the issue of informed consent on the part of the subject or patient is crucial. Yet it is not always possible to attain informed consent. In the following two chapters, we will consider subjects, or groups of subjects, with whom, for a variety of reasons, particular problems of informed consent arise. The following case is an example of such a situation, as the application of the principle of informed consent is ethically problematic. The question arises how the trial design is to be altered.

Also we need to ask if restricting informed consent might lead to paternalism on the part of the physician-researcher, and to what extent such paternalism might be justifiable.

We then consider ethical issues related to the use of women as subjects in clinical research.

This chapter concludes with a discussion on the regulations of emergency research and the problem of informed consent in this context.

The Case of saliva samples

by Salla Lötjönen[3]

The case

The A-Clinic Foundation, the National Public Health Institute and the National Research and Development Centre for Welfare and Health want to start a research project that aims to study the risk behaviour of the users of illicit intravenous drugs in Finland. They have three alternative options for conducting the study:

1) interview and taking a saliva sample with personal details as a cohort study (follow-up every half a year)
2) anonymous interview and taking a saliva sample (cross-sectional data once a year)
3) anonymous interview (cross-sectional data once a year)

The structured interviews are planned to take place at a needle exchange service and a treatment assessment unit for drug users in the capital area, and at some needle exchange services in a few Finnish cities. Pharmacies and snowball sampling are also used for recruiting. The actual interviews and sample taking would take place outside the pharmacy. First, the participants would be asked whether they would be willing to take part in alternative 1, if not, then alternative 2, and finally alternative 3. Refusal of the participant to take part in the study would naturally be respected. The number of subjects needed is 1000 to 1200.

The saliva samples would be collected using a commercially available device with indicator. The samples would be tested in the reference laboratory and the results would not be revealed to the participants. The tests could reveal the presence of HIV and/or HCV infections. As the test results would be obtained with a delay, and the saliva test is not always 100 percent reliable in discovering Hepatitis C, the researchers would view the results as not attractive for use in individual

3 I would like to thank Prof. Pauli Leinikki, of the National Institute of Public Health, Finland, for making this case available to me.

diagnostics. Those interested in the results would be encouraged to use other channels to find out their infectious status. Tests are available free of charge in all health centres and in some specific testing and counselling sites.

All the details would be kept strictly confidential, with the consent forms containing personal details from alternative 1 kept in a safe at the A-Clinic Foundation. Personal details would only be linked to the saliva samples by a code sticker, which is also attached to the consent form. In alternatives 2 and 3, the second letters of the first and last name with the second figure of the day of birth (e.g., AO8) would be used for controlling overlapping samples that could cause bias.

Activity:

Try to imagine the very difficult situation of a drug user: the addiction to drugs, the mental, social and financial problems, and so on. And then imagine such a person being asked to participate in the trial described above. How would a drug user probably react?

Ethical and legal considerations of the case

According to Finnish law, a person cannot be recruited into clinical research without giving written consent and without the approval of a multidisciplinary ethics committee. Technical details are given by decree and are defined according to current interpretation among experts. Whenever a biological sample is collected, the study is then regarded as clinical research and a written consent with the subject's full identification is required. As the participants are users of illicit drugs, it is thought that not many of them would be willing to give their personal details, although they would be ensured of confidentiality. Because of the provision for written consent, the ethics committee has taken the position of not allowing the collection of a saliva sample anonymously from persons who would otherwise be willing to provide a sample. This position of the committee endangers the study, which is of utmost importance as the cases of AIDS are increasing in Finland, and the authorities need accurate information on the present situation as soon as possible.

Activity:

Is the decision of the researchers not to disclose the results of the saliva tests to the subjects ethical? Should the subjects be able to choose whether or not they want to know the results? Is there enough of a public health concern here to make it preferable for the possible carriers of the virus to be made aware of their condition?

Further, the questionnaire used for the interview includes questions of a very personal nature, such as questions on sexual behaviour, social background, whether the subject has served time in prison, habits of using illicit drugs and so on. If the interview is also interpreted as violating the integrity of the person, then the interview could not be conducted without written consent of the subject as well. Identification could then have the same potentially harmful effect to recruiting the subjects as described above. One might, however, ask whether the requirement of written consent will have a negative effect on recruiting in the end. After all, the most likely venues for recruiting are the counselling sites where the clients are already coming forward. On the other hand, not getting any recruits from outside the counselling venues could present an inaccurate reading of the present situation. Additionally, in a worst case scenario, asking people to take part in research in which they are required to provide personal information may turn off the drug users from making contact with the counselling services altogether.

This case illustrates that although written consent is fundamentally ethically positive, insisting on attaining it in all circumstances causes ethical problems. In the following section, a commentary on this case is presented, in which an interesting alternative is proposed to allow the research to be performed while still observing the legal requirements of obtaining written consent.

In his commentary, P. Wainwright discusses the options in the initial stages of the case study and focuses on the problem of anonymising the research subjects. Another ethical problem presented is the decision of the researchers not to communicate the results of the test to the subjects. Is there any justification for not notifying them?

Commentary on the case

by Paul Wainwright

Research involving any group of subjects who engage in unlawful activity such as illicit drug use inevitably raises issues of anonymity and confidentiality and may place both the researcher and the subject in a difficult position. However, given the importance of the research and the ways in which clients such as drug users are normally protected from the legal consequences of their actions when in the health care setting, it would seem reasonable for the researchers to offer anonymity to potential recruits to the study. Anonymity would make it impossible to conduct a cohort study, but would not entirely compromise the value of the research as it would still be useful to gather general information about risk behaviour and levels of infection in an anonymous group.

Let us have a look at the options at the beginning of the case study. The anonymous testing proposed in option 2 (anonymous interview and taking a saliva sample, cross-sectional data once a year) is not necessarily a good approach. One might question whether samples from anonymous individuals, as opposed to anonymised samples from known individuals, are actually a good idea.

A comparison could be drawn with the anonymised testing of pregnant women for HIV. In this instance, in the United Kingdom, women who entered the maternity care system because they were pregnant had a blood sample taken to test for HIV, the intention being to establish the incidence of HIV infection in that population. However, the blood sample had all forms of identity removed before it was tested.

In other cases, tissue banks have been established for genetic research. The tissue samples are collected from known individuals with a particular clinical history, of Type II diabetes, for example, but the link between sample and individual subject is irrevocably broken before the tissue sample can be included in the bank.

In both these examples, the tissue sample came from a known individual with an established clinical history, even though, subsequently, we cannot know (short of DNA comparisons) which particular individual the sample came from. This seems acceptable, because the research interest is in the characteristics of the population, rather than the characteristics of any individual. It is actually desirable that the researchers do not know which individual any given sample originated from, only that it came from one member of a known group.

However, in option 2 of this research proposal the suggestion is that samples be collected from anonymous individuals. We are led to believe that the typical individual is a drug user (to be fair, given that the person was recruited through the Drug Counselling Service or needle exchange service, we are pretty certain that the person is a user), but we cannot ever be absolutely sure.

The subjects' status as drug users is something they are apparently willing to be open about, because they attend the drug counselling service. Even if they are allowed to maintain their anonymity when they access the counselling service, if the authorities wished to do so they could presumably raid the clinic, or wait outside to observe those who use it. Subjects may, however, understandably be reluctant to have data about lifestyle, risk behaviour, and HIV or Hepatitis C infection linked to them in an identifiable way. An alternative approach might be to ask subjects to give their personal details but to ensure that these were then separated from the data.

Activity:

Wainwright provides a solution which respects the law, and which also takes into account the researchers' interests, as well as protecting the interests of drug users. Do you find this solution convincing or do you still see other problems? Does it remove the barriers to the drug users' participation in the research?

In the following section, option 1 will also be critically considered.

One more ethical issue is worth considering. In option 1 of the proposed study, involving subjects who are willing to give consent and thus be identified, it is proposed that personal identifiers would be removed from samples, which would be identified by means of a code sticker that would also be attached to the consent form. Data would thus be kept confidential, but not anonymous. However, the results of the tests would not be communicated to the subjects. This raises two questions.

The first is that the researchers will be in possession of information about the HIV and HCV status of the subjects. For those subjects who are found to be HIV or HCV positive, is there not an ethical duty to ensure that those subjects are given proper counselling, access to treatment services, and so on? It is suggested that, because the HCV test is not 100 percent reliable, the results would not be of value to the subjects. However, few tests are 100 percent reliable, and this one is presumably thought to be sufficiently reliable for the purposes of research into the levels of Hepatitis C infection in the sample population, so this would not seem to be sufficient justification for not notifying the subject. No justification is given for not notifying subjects of their HIV status. It could be argued that, once health care personnel are in possession of information about an individual's positive HIV status, there is a duty to the individual, and to other persons who might be affected, to make that information known to the individual.

Activity:

Thus we return to the question the author of the case study raised: Is the researcher's decision not to disclose the results of the saliva tests to the subjects ethical? Taking into account the arguments you have just read, would you answer the question in the same way as you did before?

The second point concerns the stigma of the HIV test itself. Many institutions are interested in whether an individual has ever had an HIV test, the most obvious being the insurance industry. As long as the subjects' samples are identifiable then it could be argued that their answer to the question 'Have you ever had an HIV test?' must be 'Yes'. This could have adverse consequences for the individual and others close to him or her. If samples were truly anonymised prior to testing the answer to the question could reasonably be 'No'. Samples have been tested, but it is not true to say that people have been tested. No one would be in possession of any information regarding the HIV or HCV status of the individuals involved in the study. The same principle could be extended to the questionnaire data, which we are told is of a personal and intrusive nature.

It could thus be argued that the most acceptable way forward would be to try to recruit subjects who were willing to give informed consent, with the assurance that all data would be irrevocably anonymised. This could even extend to a separation of the consent process from the data collection, one researcher taking the consent and a different individual conducting the interview and collecting the saliva sample. Only if a serious attempt at recruitment on this basis failed would it be necessary to consider going to option 2.

The ethical issues here concern the need to protect the individual's dignity and the interests of the vulnerable group without behaving in a patronising and paternalistic manner.

Is this problem exclusive to vulnerable groups? To what extent is paternalism also a problem with respect to 'normal' subjects? Can a sensible form of paternalism also exist? These questions will be pursued in the following article by P. Wainwright.

Wainwright points out that in everyday life we allow people to engage in many dangerous pursuits, but, in the area of health care research, the opposite appears to be true. This observation points out the problem of the relationship between the doctrine of informed consent and paternalism. Wainwright describes how both terms should be defined, and which problem involving consent can arise in practice. Is the protection of research subjects only possible through the tension occurring between informed consent and paternalism?

Paternalism versus informed consent: Issues in research ethics

by Paul Wainwright

Introduction

Paternalism in the discussion of health care ethics for the United Kingdom has acquired rather a bad name. The idea that health care professionals might make decisions that they perceive to be in the best interests of a patient, on the basis of their professional expertise, without taking proper account of the patient's autonomous right to make an informed choice, is generally understood as unacceptable. We are frequently reminded that, even when the patient's choice might appear to us to be irrational, it is nevertheless his or her right to make such a choice and such a choice must be respected. Thus we have the British Medical Association reminding practitioners that advance refusals to life-saving treatment should be respected, and British courts ruling that even patients detained under the Mental Health Act have the right to refuse surgery, without which they are more than likely to die (Re C [1994] 1 All ER [= All England Law Reports] 819). The Declaration of Helsinki (→ Appendix 3, p.123), in the context of medical research, states:

> 22. In any research on human beings, each potential subject must be adequately informed of the aims, methods, sources of funding, any possible conflicts of interest, institutional affiliations of the researcher, the anticipated benefits and potential risks of the study and the discomfort it may entail. The subject should be informed of the right to abstain from participation in the study or to withdraw consent to participate at any time without reprisal. After ensuring that the subject has understood the information, the physician should then obtain the subject's freely-given informed consent, preferably in writing. If the consent cannot be obtained in writing, the non-written consent must be formally documented and witnessed.

In everyday life we allow people to engage in many dangerous pursuits, such as going to sea in small boats, mountain climbing, flying, free-fall parachuting, hang gliding, diving, driving fast cars or motorcycles, consuming alcohol and tobacco, or engaging in risky sexual activities, all with the minimum of constraints. We can risk all our money on ill-advised investments, or by betting on horse races or buying lottery tickets. In a liberal democracy the extent to which the State restricts the potentially self-harming activities of the individual is relatively limited.

However, in the area of health care research, the opposite appears to be true. Although it might appear that the emphasis is on patient information and informed consent, it can in fact be argued that the Research Ethics Committee process is a particular form of paternalism. In this paper it will be argued that paternalism of this kind is justified and is in fact an important and necessary safeguard for the protection of vulnerable individuals.

Paternalism and the Doctrine of Informed Consent

Downie and Calman (1987) define paternalism as follows:

> the protection of individuals from self inflicted harm, in the way that a father or mother looks after children. Decisions are taken, choices made and freedom inhibited, all for the good of the patient. There is no element of consent ... Above all, paternalism is shown in the taking of decisions for others which they have a right to take for themselves ... above all it is an offence against autonomy (pp. 144–45).

They suggest that paternalism is 'patronising and hurtful because it conveys that the patient is not capable of understanding anything, or that the patient is too unimportant to be worth the trouble of an explanation' (p. 96), and they go on to say that 'health care professionals ... may simply believe that they know more about what the patient does, thinks or feels than the patient himself' (p. 97).

Activity:

Do you know of actual examples of paternalism in the regulation of health research in your own country?

Accounts of paternalism stress the damaging effects of ignoring or overriding individual autonomy, liberty and privacy. Such accounts are generally based in Lockean notions of personhood and Kantian accounts of autonomy.

The Kantian injunction that persons must never be used merely as means to an end is taken up by Edwards (2000), who points out that we are nevertheless allowed to use others as means to achieving our own ends when those others have freely consented to this. Thus we may 'use' all manner of professionals and trades people for our own ends so long as the people concerned have freely chosen their occupation for their own ends, even if in doing so such people thus used are exposed to the risk of harm: 'It is morally legitimate for individuals to undergo harms (or risk of harms) for the sakes of others providing they choose so to do' (Edwards 2000: 71). Consent thus becomes the standard defence against accusations that we are using people merely as means to an end.

Hewlett (1996: 233) takes this further, in the context of research, and argues that informed consent

> ... is an autonomous authorisation by one person to permit another person to carry out an agreed procedure which affects the subject and therefore by asking patients to consent to research, we respect their wishes, enable them to be self-governing and uphold the principle of respect for persons.

However, it is not always quite as simple as it sounds. Many commentators have discussed the difficulties of obtaining a proper, valid consent, even from a competent, well-informed individual.

Activity:

In earlier sections of this book we have already considered such difficulties. Return to the example in the article about consent and inducement presented by R. Ashcroft (see p. 21). To what extent was attaining proper, valid consent made more difficult?

Problems with consent

It is generally accepted that human subjects in medical research can be described as vulnerable. Evans and Evans (1996) make this the starting point for their discussion of research ethics and argue that the status of the medical profession and medicine in general is likely to influence the desire of potential research subjects to be seen to be doing something of importance. Patients frequently have a sense of obligation, and want to be seen to be cooperative. Edwards (2000) argues that such factors may be even stronger among people with intellectual disabilities and appeals for a category of hyper-vulnerability to describe such people. Even if patients were to feel no sense of obligation or desire to cooperate, and were in full possession of their intellectual faculties we might still question the basis of consent for participating in research. The complexities of research design are such that even expert researchers will disagree about the value of one method over another and what will count as good science (see, for example, the recent debate about the need for placebo arms in clinical trials in Rothman and Michels 1994, 2000; Macklin 1999; Weijer 1999; Baum 2000), so the extent to which consent can ever be 'informed' must be deemed limited.

Macklin (1999: 994) refers to patients falling prey to the 'therapeutic misconception' which, she says, is 'the all-too-common assumption that research promises beneficial treatment, even in its earliest phases'. She goes on to report that:

> In one study, people who had been research subjects told interviewers that they had trusted their doctors, believed that their physicians would do nothing to harm them, and thought that the physician-researchers had always acted in their best medical interests. The misconception that research is designed to benefit the patients who are the subjects is difficult to dispel (p. 994).

This kind of evidence, says Macklin, suggests 'that the informed consent process remains imperfect' and that 'experience provides evidence that the protection of human subjects cannot rest solely on the ethical foundation of informed consent'.

Activity:

What circumstances would make research subjects believe that their physicians would do nothing to harm them and that the physician-researchers had always acted in their best medical interests?

Make a list of possible ways in which a patient can be mislead:

For example, the research takes place in a hospital, etc.

Other pressures apart from patients' misguided trust in their doctors may also be relevant. Clinical research involves substantial sums of money and holds out the prospect of personal advancement for those who conduct it and prestige for the institutions involved. Not surprisingly, this places considerable pressure on researchers. A recent editorial (Anon 2000) in *The Lancet* reviews a US Government report that found the following:

> ... in the race to enrol trial participants, many recruiters in the USA are adopting practices that seem to compromise patients' confidentiality, abuse the doctor-patient relationship, and ignore basic requirements for informed consent. Although the report focused on industry-sponsored trials, ...investigators said similar practices are occurring in trials backed by government agencies and other non-commercial sponsors (p. 2177).

The report notes the startling growth in the number of trials being performed and the equally sharp increase in the number of subjects recruited per trial, noting that 'In the early 1980s the average number of individuals included for new drug application trials was 1,321. By the early 1990s that number had more than tripled to 4,237'. The cost of developing drugs has also increased dramatically, from around $50 million per drug in the 1970s to as much as $500 million today, so there is also pressure to bring new products to market as quickly as possible.

The Protection of vulnerable human subjects

Bauman suggests that one of the great issues of ethics is the 'synchronisation of individual conduct and collective welfare' (1993: 4). In the context of medical research, it could be argued that collective welfare, on the one hand, demands a thriving and well-supported programme of clinical research, in the interests of improved health, well-being and longevity. However, this must be balanced against another aspect of collective welfare, the protection from exploitation of those on whom this programme of research would be conducted. Individual conduct, though, demands that those engaged in health care research and the health care industries have the freedom and encouragement to pursue their trades without undue restraint, and that those who would, for whatever reason, offer themselves as research subjects are likewise given appropriate encouragement and not unreasonably constrained.

Activity:

Do you agree with this model of 'synchronisation of individual conduct and collective welfare'? Is a balance between individual conduct and collective welfare possible and is this of ethical worth? Would giving appropriate encouragement to people to apply as research subjects actually support collective welfare rather than individual conduct?

It was noted in the introduction to this paper that in other spheres of life we allow and even encourage people to take quite severe risks in or with their lives. Freedom of choice that precludes the right to make dangerous choices is no freedom at all. But as Macklin (1999: 994) states,

> ... researchers have an obligation to minimize the risks to their subjects, and institutional review boards are charged with ensuring that the risks are reasonable in the light of the anticipated benefits. There would be no need for a system of institutional review boards to protect subjects if their informed consent were the only ethical requirement for conducting research.

Macklin's comment introduces a shift of emphasis. To return to everyday life, there may be nothing to stop me from buying a new hang-glider and jumping off a cliff with it, but there are considerable restrictions on those who manufacture and sell hang-gliders, to ensure that they are constructed by an acceptable standard. Less dramatically, when I board a train or a plane for a journey, I know I am accepting a degree of risk, but I also know that the train company and the airline operate under strict regulations, so as to minimise that risk. Events like the Hatfield and Paddington train crashes of 1999 and 2000 in the United Kingdom have demonstrated the level of concern generated by any mishap that might be attributable to a failure on the part of the operators to maintain an acceptable safety culture. It is not my freedom to take risks that is being threatened but the freedom of others to take risks with me. In the interests of public policy, a complex system of regulation has been set up to prevent unreasonable risks being taken with the lives of others. This system of regulation is one way that government can manage 'the synchronisation of individual conduct and collective welfare'. The temptation on the part of individuals to cut corners in order to maximise profit, even though that increases the risk to passengers or customers or the general public, is counterbalanced in the name of collective welfare by legislation.

Activity:

Return once more to the beginning of this section. Here it is stated that one of the great issues in ethics is the 'synchronisation of individual conduct and collective welfare'. Hence, we have a system of regulations that are intended to protect patients or customers from unreasonable risks.

What are the advantages and dangers of a complex system of regulation of medical research?

What do you think about a physician-researcher who is claiming: 'I act ethically correctly, because I comply with all the regulations'?

Conclusion

Strong accounts of paternalism, such as those quoted above from Downie and Calman, emphasise the denial of autonomy, with decisions being taken by others that rightfully belong to the competent individual agent. It is not suggested in this paper that the system of REC (research ethics committee) review represents strong paternalism in this sense. However, the regulation of clinical research does involve decisions being taken, choices being made and freedom being inhibited, for the good of the research subject. It may not be true that there is no element of consent, but the range of risks and harms to which potential research subjects are allowed to consent is limited. In the legal system of the United Kingdom, at least, it is not generally thought to be in the public interest for individuals to consent to certain forms of personal harm or injury to be inflicted on them by others. Restrictions of this sort can be seen as a form of paternalism, albeit a weak form. Given the nature of research and the range of interests driving the research agenda, a degree of paternalism of this nature seems entirely appropriate.

Activity:

The first activity of this article asked about the possible paternalism in the regulation system in your country. How would you assess this system? Are more or fewer regulations needed in your view?

The issue of paternalism is also presented in the next article concerning the use of women as subjects in clinical research. Over the last twenty-five years a change has occurred. Previously, the participation of women in clinical trials was considered problematic due to the specific risks involved. Now, the under-representation of women in trials can be seen as discriminatory.

M. Jones deals with the issue of whether or not women should be used in clinical trials. She describes the background of this issue in the United States and considers the general question of whether or not any appropriate individual has the right or even a duty to participate in clinical trials. The general debate about the use of human subjects in research centres on the more concrete problem of informed consent. Women are asked to agree not to conceive at least for the period of the trial and to take contraceptives. Jones makes clear that the use of contraceptives within the framework of clinical trials involves problematic ethical dimensions. The problem of contraceptives is especially relevant in the case of a drug such as thalidomide, which has recognisable benefits for women as well as teratogenic effects. A further problem regarding women in a clinical trial is the process by which they are selected and the right of the investigator to refuse a woman's request to participate in a clinical trial.

Ethical issues surrounding the use of women as subjects in clinical research

by Melanie Jones

The issue of whether or not women should be used in clinical trials is a complex and relatively new one, in that prior to thalidomide (Contergan®), there were in fact few restrictions to women's participation in such activities. However, the teratogenic effects of thalidomide were so severe that in 1977 the US Food and Drug Administration (FDA) introduced legislation which effectively excluded the majority of 'women of reproductive potential' from participation in early clinical trials (Food and Drug Administration 77–3040).

Changes in disease patterns, and a growing awareness that many of the drugs licensed for use in the United States had never been tested on women, have brought further changes in legislation in recent years. In particular, the advent of AIDS has led to suggestions that women should be encouraged to participate in clinical trials and that, furthermore, data should be gathered which make clear the effects of drugs, given factors such as age, gender, class and ethnicity. A re-examination of whether and how women should be used in clinical trials was prompted in part by the fact that in attempts by the WHO (World Health Organisation) and UNAIDS to identify cheaper treatments for AIDS for use in developing countries, many pregnant women were used in trials for AZT in an endeavour to reduce the rate of maternal transmission of the disease. The case proved controversial. The refusal of the investigators to use 'historical controls' derived from the trials of the previously licensed *zidovudine* led to the premature deaths of many babies (Schüklenk 2000). But the reality of AIDS brought to researcher's attention the need to discuss how women could be admitted to such studies for their own benefit.

The trial, undertaken in developing countries, was, as stated, very controversial. Is it morally right to test treatments for AIDS with placebo-controlled studies? Some argued that historical controls would have sufficed. An objection was that placebo-controlled trials lead faster to statistically predictive results, and that no woman participating in these studies was worse off than she would have been had she not participated. It has to be taken into account that women involved in the trials described above would have been unable to afford an AZT intervention in any case.

This new appraisal of women involved in clinical studies is linked to a general increase in data collection and storage. While the US guidelines are clear, they are also unambiguous about their own need for more complete data. In 1993 the FDA recommended that women of all ages should be included in trials and for the results to be analysed by gender: it is now the case that all New Drug Applications must be accompanied by an analysis of data for demographic subgroups such as age, gender, class and ethnicity (Office for Protection from Research Risks 93–4).

Ethical issues

There is little argument about whether women should participate in clinical trials for drugs which are sex-specific, such as Hormone Replacement Therapy (HRT) or breast cancer treatments, but concerns are often voiced about whether or not women should take part in trials of general, non-sex-specific treatments. For the purposes of this paper, I wish to examine the inclusion of women in non-sex-specific drug trials. But where the literature indicates that it is helpful, I shall refer to examples from both types of trials, since drug trials tailored for women only are sometimes useful in ascertaining the stance of women themselves towards participation in such activity.

General rights and duties

The first ethical question to be addressed is that of whether or not any appropriate individual has a right to participate in a clinical trial, or indeed, whether there is a duty towards others to do so. Schüklenk (2000) suggests that current approaches towards the use of particular demographic groups in clinical trials are underpinned by two distinctive philosophical traditions. Firstly, he refers to utilitarian concepts, where both individual action and public policy should maximise utility for the greatest number of people, and where consequences are used as the exclusive criteria for action. Secondly, he identifies deontological concepts, which suggest that duty should motivate morally appropriate action, driven by principle, rather than by knowledge of the consequence of the action, and furthermore, that autonomy has its own intrinsic value.

Some writers (e.g., Tobias 1997) argue that patients have a duty to participate in clinical research and to trust doctors to make decisions about such matters on their behalf. He suggests that informed consent from the patient should not always be required, particularly where the difficulties of explaining the nature of the consent are likely to deter both doctors and patients from participating. Tobias's argument is radically utilitarian. The notion of informed consent, however, carries particular meaning when women capable of childbearing participate in clinical trials.

Activity:

Arguing that patients have a duty to participate in clinical research may sound very restrictive and authoritarian. What could support such a requirement? What would be the arguments against it?

Informed consent

The debate about the nature of informed consent necessarily underpins any debate about the use of human subjects in clinical trials, but has particular pertinence for women because of the risks of teratogenesis (risk or potential risk of reproductive toxicity). In the United States, there is a basic safety net in existence in that the Belmont Report advocates that no research should be undertaken using women of childbearing potential if there are known to be possible teratogenic effects, and a similar position is held in Britain and Europe. But there is nevertheless a possibility that some non-sex-specific drugs may produce such effects, however mild.

Women in the United States and in Europe are asked to agree not to conceive for the period of the trial and are sometimes also warned that the effects of the treatment may continue for a period after the trial is complete. Guidelines in the United States advise that 'women and men can eliminate the possibility of pregnancy through abstinence and reduce the possibility of pregnancy through the use of contraception for the duration of drug exposure (which may exceed the length of the study)' and that they should discuss this with their sexual partner before deciding to participate (Food and Drug Administration 1997: 21 CFR 312). In Britain, women (and pubescent girls in studies that include subjects in this age group) are asked to take precautions not to conceive during the period of a study and, sometimes regardless of whether or not they are sexually active or of their sexuality, to take contraceptive precautions. The FDA suggests that women should be 'required', if necessary, to use contraception and that an IRB can also 'require' pregnancy testing to be carried out prior to the study, at intervals during the study, and after the study.

While there are concerns, then, about the possibility of teratogenesis, these do not, in general, extend to men. In trials of sex-specific drugs for men which are known to have possible teratogenic effects, it is not uncommon to ask men to take measures regarding the use of contraception, but in trials for non-sex-specific drugs, it seems to be a question which is rarely addressed. Contraception is not an issue without ethical dimensions, and the right to insist on women participants in clinical trials to take contraception has ramifications for women of many persuasions, not least of all for Roman Catholic women and women from minority ethnic groups. Therefore, the imperative to protect them from harm excludes some women from participation in trials, since to participate would require adopting contraceptive practices that would not be in keeping with their moral or religious viewpoint. This militates against the requirement to ensure that the benefits and burdens of research are distributed fairly.

Activity:

Is it morally right to require women to take contraceptives? For example, if a woman with a severe disease wants to take part in a trial, because she expects to benefit from the trial, but refuses to take contraceptives for religious or other reasons, should she be excluded? Or should it be up to the woman (and possibly her partner) to decide whether or not to take contraceptives, and whether or not to run the risks of the trial?

Teratogenesis

There is little evidence to indicate what the outcome would be should a woman become pregnant during the period of the trial. This example would be relevant in the case if a drug such as thalidomide (Contergan®), which has known teratogenic effects, but the use of which is also known to produce recognisable benefits in other areas of treatment, notably, in the treatment of leprosy. The advice of the FDA (45 CFR 46 1991 Code of Federal Regulations: Protection of Human Subjects, Department of Health and Human Services [DHHS], National Institutes of Health [NIH], Office for Protection from Research Risks [OPRR]) is as follows:

1) 'individuals engaged in the activity (clinical research) will have no part in any decisions as to the timing, method and procedures used to terminate the pregnancy and
2) determining the viability of the foetus at the termination of pregnancy.'

Whilst such regulations protect women from potentially unscrupulous action by investigators, the implication of such statements by default is that institutions or organisations are not debarred from putting pressure on a woman in such a context.

Should a pregnant woman be involved in a trial for a treatment which is deemed to be in her interests to take, and which poses low risk to the foetus, a partner's consent will be required unless:

1) Participation is purely in the interests of the health of the mother
2) The partner cannot be found
3) The partner is not reasonably available
4) The woman has been raped

This brings into question a father's rights over his unborn offspring and a mother's right to make autonomous decisions regarding her own health and well-being.

There is little evidence to indicate what would actually happen in the United States should a woman become pregnant during a clinical trial or whether investigators would be in a position to enforce a termination of the pregnancy, although it seems unlikely. Informal inquiries made to research managers working in drug companies in the United Kingdom produced somewhat guarded accounts, but it was acknowledged that sometimes 'it happens'. Research managers suggested that the usual course of action would be to follow the woman throughout pregnancy, check the baby for abnormalities when born and, provided the baby was healthy, discontinue contact with the mother. However, no clear protocol or legislation could be cited by those questioned. Further anecdotal evidence from e-mail discussion groups in the United States suggests that should this situation arise during a trial there, investigators would require access to the child for at least a year after its birth. There are some central questions here about the State's rights over the individual that seem to call into question the principle of respect for persons, but further evidence is required.

Selection of women for trials

There is evidence to suggest that women are not uniformly used for clinical trials. This occurs for a number of reasons. The notion of informed consent affects the selection process, since the nature of the consent required is often complex and middle-class women, who are often perceived to be more articulate, and may indeed have a greater likelihood of more elements of shared language with an investigator and a history of a greater degree to exposure to esoteric language, do not necessarily receive the same treatments as their working class counterparts. Britton et al.(1998), in a systematic review of randomised controlled trials (RCTs) of a range of treatments, found that working-class and middle-class women were differently represented in trials and that the process of randomisation does not best serve working-class women. They report:

> Participation in RCTs differed between studies of treatment interventions (subjects tended to be less affluent, less educated and more severely ill and therefore had greater capacity to benefit from treatment) and those evaluating preventive interventions (more affluent, better educated and generally healthier and therefore had less potential to benefit than eligible subjects who declined to participate (Britton et al. 1998: 3).

Britton et al. (1998) suggest that the process of randomisation does not necessarily produce the most equitable outcomes, because those who stand to gain the most from participation in trials are often excluded by the process of randomisation. They argue that targeting vulnerable populations would help to address this imbalance. Without targeting, they suggest, investigators cannot rightly extrapolate from their data to populations.

There are difficulties in treating any demographic subgroup as a homogenous group without cross cutting interests. 'Women' form a category, which cannot be viewed entirely independently of factors such as age, class and ethnicity. While the FDA is explicit about its need for data, without cross tabulation of the data for the different subgroups, the data remain, at best, crude. My enquiries of drug company research managers in the United Kingdom suggested that while information is collected with regard to gender, it is rarely collected with regard to social class, and cross tabulated data are not available. It should be borne in mind, however that such cross tabulation, has its own ethical connotations, particularly where the research is in the field of genetics. Nevertheless, as Britton et al. (1998) suggest, participation in trials is by no means even.

Activity:

Do you agree with the suggestion that information should be collected not only with regard to gender, but also with regard to social class? What problems could arise if this were done? Would this measure encourage the dividing of society in social classes, although the intention is the opposite?

Exclusion

Investigators still hold the right to refuse a woman's request to participate in a clinical trial. Informal discussions with research managers from drug companies suggested that their role in the conduct of the trial is in fact minimal and that most of the major decisions are left to local investigators. If, for example, a woman is deemed by an investigator likely to be unreliable where the use of contraception is concerned, she will not be assigned to the trial. It hardly needs to be said that there are likely to be class assumptions here, which mirror those in the section on selection procedures and that, because of such factors, women may be under-represented in trials of some treatments. The question here is of whether there is any intrinsic right to take part in a clinical trial, especially given that it may improve a woman's chances of recovery. The issue of incentives is pertinent here: identifying research subjects can be a lucrative business for doctors and, it could be argued, the fact that remuneration is often received could encourage the doctors to be less inclined to exclude subjects on grounds such as poor contraceptive practice.

The problem of informed consent beyond the western concept of autonomy

While I do not wish to enter the debate on, for example, 'race' and clinical trials, a letter that appeared in the British Medical Journal (Cullinan 1997) prompts one final speculation. Tim Cullinan, Head of the Community Health Department at the University of Malawi, asserts that the western concept of autonomy, which is enshrined in the principle of informed consent, is a concept derived from a 'shaky Judaeo-Christian-Liberal ethic'. He maintains that whereas in the west, our philosophy is underpinned by the tenet cogito, ergo sum ('I think, therefore I am'), in many traditional African cultures, the individual takes his or her autonomy from sumus, ergo sum ('we are, therefore I am'). Cullinan suggests:

> In many parts of Africa it is simply not possible, especially for women, to make important decisions without reference to the group; any clinician or researcher who believes that a 'yes' given by a terrified and lonely patient, in or out of a hospital bed, amounts to anything approaching informed consent is either naïve or a knave. Add this to the very real social difficulty in ever saying 'no' and thus threatening a relationship and you have the perfect situation for doing everything you like (1997: 248).

This suggests that notions such as informed consent are culture-bound to a degree and that increasing globalisation will necessitate the patient's perspective being addressed in a broader cultural sense.

The social and ethical concepts of various cultures around the world do not seem compatible. The problem already arises within one culture alone. It is the aim of European researchers to come to an agreement on guidelines for medical research. The next article not only deals with the Declaration of Helsinki, but also with the European Convention on Human Rights and Biomedicine.

One important but also problematic area of medical research has been created by the development of emergency treatments. Such treatments must be tested for efficacy on patients in emergency situations. As many emergency patients are incapable of giving their informed consent, special regulations are needed to protect them. S. Lötjönen discusses these issues in the following article.

Clinical research in emergency settings

by Salla Lötjönen[4]

Since the Nuremberg trials (1945–50) and the creation of the Nuremberg Code (→ Appendix 1, p.108), the requirement of free and informed consent has been accepted as the corner-

4 The following paper is a modified version of Lötjönen, S. 2002. Medical research in clinical emergency settings in Europe. *Journal of Medical Ethics* 28(3):183–7 (with permission from the BMJ Publishing Group).

stone of any medical research or experimentation involving human beings. Some claim that research on persons with diminished capacity to give consent should be conducted under very strict conditions only, and never without the approval of a legal representative (Höfling and Demel 1999). Medical experimentation on incapacitated persons has been called into question for its violation not only of personal autonomy but also of human rights (Medical research involving incapacitated persons. Report to the Minister ... the Netherlands 1995). If research on children and mentally incapacitated persons with proxy consent is considered problematic, then what about medical research on unconscious patients who enter the Emergency and Accident Ward without any accompanying persons able to state either the patient's identity or his or her views on participating in research?

Emergency settings occur not only under conditions entailing severe trauma, but also in situations involving cardiac arrest, acute congestive heart failure, sepsis or haemorrhage, stroke or drug overdose. Patients suffering from these conditions can hardly be expected to read a multipage information sheet describing the nature and purpose of proposed research as well as all the risks and benefits that could be involved, even if the patients were conscious. Therefore, requiring a standard informed consent procedure can be on many occasions completely out of the question, even if such an enforced standard is always to be preferred. However, emergency patients, at high risk of morbidity or death, might be in greatest need of novel therapies and might be willing to assume some risk for a potential benefit.

If the efficacy of certain treatments for these conditions cannot be tested on healthy subjects and the nature of these conditions undermines the capacity of the patient-subjects themselves, the only options for conducting research in this situation are either to gain informed consent from a legal representative, or to proceed with experimentation without any consent until such is made available. In fact, trials in emergency situations have been conducted both in the United States and in Europe using various consent designs. In the United States, the Food and Drug Administration (FDA) and the Department of Health and Human Services (HHS) gave out waivers of informed consent for emergency research on October 2, 1996 (61 FR 51498-51531, 21CFR 50.24). In Europe, such regulation is still under development. Nevertheless, the need for such research remains the same on both continents and, therefore, an ethical and legal analysis on research in emergency settings is needed also in Europe.

Despite the inadequate level of detail, some guidance already exists that concerns medical research in emergency settings both globally and at the European level. The recently revised Declaration of Helsinki (→ Appendix 3, p.123) states:

> 26. Research on individuals from whom it is not possible to obtain consent, including proxy or advance consent, should be done only if the physical/mental condition that prevents obtaining informed consent is a necessary characteristic of the research population. The specific reasons for involving research subjects with a condition that renders them unable to give informed consent should be stated in the experimental protocol for consideration and approval of the review committee. The protocol should state that consent to remain in the research should be obtained as soon as possible from the individual or a legally authorised surrogate.

The Declaration of Helsinki states many of the conditions that are relevant when conducting research in emergency settings, although a global professional guideline cannot, obviously, be very specific. However, some basic conditions can be extracted from the text:

1) research cannot be conducted using other research participants capable of giving informed consent;
2) research shall be adequately planned and designed in a research protocol;
3) protocol shall be approved by an ethics committee for emergency conditions specifically;
4) informed consent is not obtainable:
   a) from the participant him or herself when the circumstances for research are at hand,
   b) from the participant him or herself previously,
   c) from his or her legally authorised representative;
5) informed consent for continued participation in the trial shall be obtained from either the participant him or herself or the legal representative as soon as possible.

All of the requirements listed above are necessary if research in emergency settings is to be ethically justified according to the Declaration of Helsinki. An almost identical list of criteria can be extracted from the International Conference on Harmonisation Good Clinical Practice (ICH GCP) guidelines drafted as an international ethical and scientific quality standard for trials on medicinal products (CPMP/ICH/135/95). However, neither the Declaration nor the ICH GCP describes the nature of research that may be conducted without a proxy consent, i.e., what kind of research may be conducted if the conditions above have been fulfilled. Additionally, as both the Declaration of Helsinki and the ICH GCP lack direct legal effect, more guidance should be sought from the Council of Europe Convention on Human Rights and Biomedicine.

Activity:

Try to find out the position on proxy decision makers in the legal system of your own country.

The most prominent legal document touching the area in the European context is the Council of Europe Convention on Human Rights and Biomedicine (→ Appendix 2, p.110). Although it does not, in its present form, address emergency research specifically, most of the basic conditions set above can also be extracted from the Convention articles dealing with biomedical research (Chapter V). More particularly, Article 17 of the Convention states provisions on the protection of persons not able to consent to research. The conditions include an authorisation of a representative or an authority or a person or body provided by law. Nevertheless, it seems as if the drafters have not taken into account circumstances in which it is not possible to obtain consent from a representative due to lack of time, as no mention of emergency biomedical research is made either in the text of the Convention or in its explanatory memorandum (Explanatory Report DIR/JUR 5, paras 103–114). However, emergency situations in general (not limited to research) are addressed in Article 8, where the rule of informed consent (Article 5) has been waived. It states:

> When because of an emergency situation the appropriate consent cannot be obtained, any medically necessary intervention may be carried out immediately for the benefit of the health of the individual concerned.

There are two ways in which this article can be interpreted. On the one hand, it could be argued that as the article is not combined with the provisions that deal with scientific research (Chapter V), it should be interpreted in a narrow sense, thereby limiting its scope of application to treatment situations only (Rynning 2001: 173). On the other hand, the text of the Article itself does not refer to standard clinical practice situations, but speaks of 'any medically necessary intervention'.

Yet another argument in favour of the more liberal interpretation is that the drafters of the Council of Europe have, in their previous guidance, addressed research in emergency settings specifically. In Principle 8 of the Council of Europe Committee of Ministers Recommendation (90) 3, three conditions for this kind of research have been given: 1) the research must have been planned to be carried out in the emergency in question; 2) the systematic research plan must have been approved by an ethics committee; and finally, 3) the research must be intended for the direct health benefit of the patient.

On the basis of the above interpretation of the Convention, two additional points may be added to the ethical criteria for research in emergency settings:

6) intervention shall be carried out for the direct benefit of the patient, and
7) intervention in question must be medically necessary and can not be delayed.

Activity:

Do you find the seven ethical criteria for research in emergency settings sufficient for the protection of the patient, or would you like to add other criteria?

– 4 –

Vulnerable groups

In the previous chapter we looked at the ethical problems that occur in situations where it is not possible, or sensible, to attain fully informed consent from research subjects. In the case of the saliva samples, the requirement for written consent could endanger the performance of the experiment. In the case of patients involved in research in emergency situations, the physical condition of the patient renders fully informed consent impossible. Though one can often explain emergency research to patients after the fact, but any explanation cannot make up for the lack of consent, or fulfil the requirement for informed consent.

In this chapter we will consider case studies in which the problem of the lack of consent is intensified. In the following case of challenging behaviour, the difficulties in satisfactorily resolving the consent problem are clearly evident. In the case of Alzheimer's disease presented at the end of the chapter, further problems are addressed which can arise due to the fundamental requirement of informed consent.

In addition, this chapter considers the extent to which research with cognitively impaired persons is ethically justified. This question will be discussed in the second article of this chapter.

The Case of challenging behaviour

by Richard Ashcroft[5]

People with learning disability sometimes display what is known as 'challenging behaviour'. Challenging behaviour has

---

5 The following paper is a modified version of Ashcroft, R., B. Fraser, M. Kerr and Z. Ahmed 2001. Are antipsychotic drugs the right treatment for challenging behaviour in learning disability: The place of a randomised trial. *Journal of Medical Ethics* 27(5): 338–43 (with permission from the BMJ Publishing Group).

been defined by Emerson as culturally abnormal behaviour(s) of such intensity, frequency or duration that the physical safety of the person or others is likely to be placed in serious jeopardy, or behaviour which is likely to seriously limit the use of, or result in the person being denied access to ordinary community facilities (Emerson and Bromley 1995).

This behaviour can be managed in various ways; the most common is to prescribe antipsychotics. Behavioural therapies are also used, but the number of people trained in these techniques is relatively small. The side effects of antipsychotic medications are well-known and serious in the long term; there can also be some serious acute side effects.

A trial is proposed to determine whether the use of a particular antipsychotic medication, representative of its class, is effective in managing challenging behaviour. At present the evidence for such effectiveness is thin, and because the side effects are serious, there is uncertainty about whether the balance of risks and benefits of continuing this therapeutic strategy is reasonable. However, there may be no practicable alternative to addressing this behaviour in the majority of health care settings. It is therefore thought useful to carry out a randomised, placebo-controlled, double-blind trial to help shape prescribing and policy in this area.

In his commentary, R. Ashcroft initially examines the benefits and risks to participants in the above-mentioned trial. He does so by differentiating between the attributes of the proposed trial and those of a classically-designed trial. Ashcroft points out that there is no new treatment tested but rather that the proposed treatment is 'unevaluated'. Also, as opposed to the classical clinical trial, the proposed trial takes on the special problem of proportionality. How can we balance benefit against harm in this case? Ashcroft discusses the ethical problems which could arise in the proposed trial due to the dissimilarities appearing between it and the classical trial.

In the next section the author assumes that the antipsychotic medication is effective in controlling challenging behaviour. This leads to the question of how does the treatment achieve this effectiveness and whether it is morally right to achieve this effectiveness and to do so by way of the proposed trial. Here,

Ashcroft is considering possible justifications for the trial. In the last section he deals with the consequences of not implementing the trial and focuses on the moral question of whether a randomised controlled trial is the only or best way to change the practice of prescribing such an unevaluated medication.

Commentary on the case

by Richard Ashcroft

The following ethical questions arise in considering the proposal: what are the benefits and risks to participants involved in the trial; what are the consequences of not performing the trial.

Benefit to participants

Examining the benefits should be considered in two stages: the benefit to participants of a trial, and the benefit 'simple' of receiving antipsychotic medication as a treatment for challenging behaviour. The issues developing through an examination of the trial are more straightforward, and are discussed first. Throughout the analysis, we assume that the trial participants are adults, and that children are excluded.

Ethical aspects of the trial

The classic clinical trial consists of two features; 1) a *new* treatment is compared with a standard treatment (which in some cases is a placebo), and 2) the risks are supposed to be 'proportionate' (i.e., reasonable) to the benefits. The proposed trial differs from the classic trial in both respects.

Firstly, there is no 'new' treatment; the 'standard' treatment is novel only from an Evidence-Based Medicine viewpoint, according to which 'new' is synonymous with 'unevaluated'. An initial question arises whether the participant could be worse off for participating in the trial than he or she would otherwise be. At present, those patients, whose challenging behaviour is treated with antipsychotics, receive such a treatment because the intended benefits, sustained not only for themselves but for their caregivers as well, in controlling their behaviour outweigh the accumulative harm associated with the side effects. Assume that candidates for the trial are not psychotic, but do display challenging behaviour serious enough to qualify them for antipsychotic treatment. Such treatment is currently common, but not universal, as the cited evidence shows. In a placebo-controlled trial, if antipsychotic therapy 'works', then the participants receiving the placebo would be worse off than they normally would be. If it 'does not work', then those receiving the antipsychotics would be no worse off than usual, and those receiving the placebo would be better off than usual (at least as regards side effects). Participants in the proposed trial can be included if they are new patients not currently using antipsychotics, so that they are not missing out on treatment which has been found to be effective for them. As in the debate on trials in schizophrenia, difficulties arise when patients, who are taking medication which is effective for them, are asked to undergo randomisation or a 'wash-out' period, which may rob them of the benefits of symptom control. This issue should not arise here. Arguably equipoise is here attained with regard to which treatment is best for each newly presenting patient, and so randomisation and placebo control are not ethically problematic.

Activity:

Consider why randomisation and placebo control are not ethically problematic in this instance and fill in this tabular chart:

	Consequences for participants receiving antipsychotics	Consequences for participants receiving placebos
If therapy works		
If therapy does not work		

A second question then develops concerning proportionality. We just assumed that the side effects were reasonable, given the severity of challenging behaviour and the benefits of controlling it. But it is clear that this cannot be merely assumed. Assume now that the *intended* benefit (control of challenging behaviour) is worthwhile for the participants. How do we weigh benefit against harm in this situation? Normally we assume that patients do this for themselves when they consent to (or refuse) treatment. In the case of treating persons with challenging behaviours in a trial, we may not be able to rely on consent, for the following two reasons: 1) the capacity of the patient to consent may be diminished (both by the complexity of the trial and by his or her learning disability); 2) because the treatment is initiated in a crisis situation against the will of the patient. It may be possible to obtain consent in advance of episodes of challenging behaviour and treatment, but this could be difficult. So we must decide whether, all things considered, participating in the trial is in the best interests of the patient (Medical Research Council 1991. The ethical conduct of research on the mentally incapacitated). Since we do not know whether the intended benefit will be an actual benefit, which is why a trial is contemplated in the first place, we must concentrate on the intended benefit.

A third question is whether patients enrolled in this trial can be withdrawn from the trial if their welfare is adversely affected by the treatment they receive. Patients within the trial will be subject to a closer monitoring of their health than they usually experience, and they should have rapid access to behavioural and other treatments according to need, aside from the placebo/antipsychotic treatment they are assigned in the trial.

Ethical aspects of the treatment

Now assume that antipsychotic medication is effective in attaining the primary endpoint, that of controlling challenging behaviour. We are still left with two questions: *how* does the treatment achieve this effect, and *whether it is morally right* to achieve this effect and to do so in this way.

How the treatment achieves its effect is not clear, although the continued use of the treatment suggests that there is some relevant effect. The incidence of mental illness in people with learning disability is higher than in the general population, and it is likely that at least some 'challenging behaviour' is the behavioural expression of a mental illness crisis; consequently, in these cases it is reasonable, prima facie, to treat mental illness in this group in the same way as in other groups. For psychotic episodes, antipsychotic medication is indicated. (The therapeutic and pharmacological aspects of psychiatric treatment are outside the scope of this paper.)

However, there is a real question about the use of antipsychotic medication in patients who are not experiencing psychotic symptoms. A case needs to be made as to why this is a biologically plausible approach to managing these patients. It would be ethically questionable to proceed on the basis that 'it just works, and we do not know why' and to leave it at that. While this strategy may be temporarily justified in the absence of other treatment or of further and better information, there must be some obligation on the part of researchers to put this type of treatment on a better scientific footing. This may, of course, be a justification for the trial–if we can show no benefit or frank harm resulting from the treatment, then there may be no need to proceed any further with this treatment in theory or practice.

Activity:

Before you read further, write down your initial thoughts on the following questions: What justifications exist for the use of antipsychotic medication with patients who are not experiencing psychotic symptoms? What reasons can you give against its use? Read once more the original definition of challenging behaviour. This definition also describes the behaviour of patients with learning disability; does this influence your opinion?

In the following section, the author presents four possible justifications for the trial.

1) Challenging behaviour is clearly problematic for the caregiver and for the patient in some sense, and normally we would agree that solving problems of this kind is a good thing, and beneficial to the patient. If we can demonstrate that challenging behaviour has an organic cause, and that this is remedied by treatment, then this would be a classical justification for treating the behaviour using drug

therapy. However, where there is doubt that the behaviour has an organic cause, it is dubious whether the treatment is in the best interests of the patient. Put more strongly, if we have reason to suppose that the challenging behaviour is caused by external factors (from boredom to unhappiness, and possibly involving neglect or maltreatment), then there are serious and difficult questions to answer about the use of drug therapies. For example, it could be argued that we are merely suppressing the challenging behaviour, rather than addressing its causes. If this were true, then a consistent stress, leading to consistent challenging behaviour, would lead to long-term maintenance on antipsychotic drugs, rather than to removal or palliation of the cause of stress. The first line of justification must be the best interests of the patients themselves, normally understood to mean the 'medical best interests'. There seems to be doubt over what this means for patients in these circumstances, and over whether this treatment promotes these interests.

2) A second justification for administering the treatment might be that use of the drug is intended to prevent the patient from causing harm to him or herself or others in the short term. This is a commonly agreed upon justification for chemical or physical restraint, but it derives from the emergency nature of the circumstances (Montgomery 1997, ch.13). Only if no other means can be found to reduce the long-term risk of dangerous challenging behaviour, does drug therapy, as a last resort, become justified for long-term or routine use, and careful guidelines would be required for use. Learning-disabled people are not generally *incapable* of learning how to express emotion and how to behave appropriately (although a few very severely disabled people may be). In order to learn how to express oneself and to behave appropriately, some challenging behaviour would be expected to arise; immediate suppression of this behaviour would make learning impossible. In some cases, the constraints of limited resources placed upon the caregiver restrict the possibility of teaching learning-disabled persons to modify their behaviour. This would, however, be an argument for demanding more resources, rather than for advocating a policy of drug treatment for nonpsychotic patients, on the grounds of justice.

Fostering learning would promote the longer-term goal of attaining a good life for the learning-disabled person, through his or her developement as a moral agent able to take (some) responsibility for his or her own behaviour and well-being.

3) A third, indirect justification for use of drug therapy would be that the challenging behaviour of a patient lowers his or her chances of independent living and risks harming the relationship he or she has with a caregiver. Hence, the patient benefits from undergoing this treatment because of the positive social impact of removing the challenging behaviour. This is identical in form to the trade off that schizophrenic and bipolar disorder patients face with their medication: the side effects of the medication are considered the price one must pay in the attempt to an orderly and stable social life. As we know, many such patients do not choose to pay this price when they have a choice (although many do). In addition, this returns us to the issue of whether learning disability should be treated as a psychiatric disorder (within the terms of the United Kingdom Mental Health Act (1983), it is). There is an association between learning disability and psychotic illness, but by no means is all challenging behaviour due to the results of having such an illness. Treatment of emotional distress or social problems by psychopharmacologic means is hugely controversial at present.
4) A fourth, indirect justification for use would be that learning disability is not well understood by the public at large, that challenging behaviour in the community is not normally tolerated, and that people with learning disability as a group suffer from stigma and prejudice if the association between learning disability and challenging behaviour is thought by the ill-informed to be both common in this group and offensive. While it would be preferable to improve social understanding and tolerance, in the context of community care generally, the attempt of such may be a rather utopian dream. Hence, our only practical option may be to control the challenging behaviour as best we can, rather than try to change social attitudes toward it and toward learning-disabled people. So even if antipsychotic treatment is harmful to the individual, it may be comparatively less harmful to the individual than the

effects of stigma and intolerance attendant upon uncontrolled behaviour. This is a sensible view, although controversial, and not all interested parties agree with this response.

Activity:

The ethical aspects of the trial as well as the ethical aspects of the treatment are very complex, and it is useful to create a table in order to gain a better perspective. Use the following grid to record possible justifications for and counterarguments against the proposed trial.

Possible justifications	Contrary arguments
1.	
2.	
3.	
4.	

Now prioritise these justifications and counterarguments. Which is the most plausible to you? Which is the least plausible?

Consequences of not trialling

Our reading of the proposal is that a widespread practice is identified which is not soundly justified and not designed to protect the safety of patients, and which lacks compelling evidence for (or against) its efficacy. So the moral question then arises: is a randomised controlled trial the only or best way to change practice?

Note first of all that a clinician who regards a treatment as not beneficial to his or her patient is obliged not to use it. But the situation may be more vague: the clinician may think other treatments (for example behavioural techniques), which are not available to him or her for one reason or another, are better, but that this treatment, which is available, is still better than nothing. Or it may be that although the treatment is recognised as not ideal theoretically, nothing better is actually available at present. This would appear to be the case here, and as such would be a local, temporary justification for use. As a matter of policy, there is some obligation to evaluate whether the other treatments should be made available and to evaluate whether or not the current standard is actually better or worse than nothing. This argument may be strengthened by appeal to the diversity of opinion in the professions (clinical equipoise) and to the lack of evidence in the current research performed for this population.

Activity:

Consider the case that behavioural treatments are available and a trial should be planned to compare psychopharmacological treatment with behavioural treatment. What difficulties are to be expected in comparing such different treatments?

If the arguments about the moral status of using this kind of treatment have weight independently of the evidential arguments, then it may be that use of antipsychotics for nonpsychotic people with learning disability is morally wrong independently of their 'effectiveness'. However, analogous to clinical equipoise, it is arguable that there is a moral difference of opinion in this context, and consequently, the only reliable way to support or to change the current practice will be to complete a clinical trial.

If this is plausible, there is a further moral difficulty. It is arguable that we are using a group of patients to settle a difference of scientific opinion, and to help future patients (including these patients themselves in the future), rather than to aid these patients now. If it is morally wrong to treat these patients in this way, then we should just stop doing so. This argument can be understood through the statement made earlier in this paper: a clinician must use his or her clinical judgement. Arguably, this argument is not symmetrical: a clinician who believes that it is morally right to use this treatment must meet a higher standard of proof, because he or she must further show that the treatment works. The clinician who morally objects arguably does not need to demonstrate further that the treatment does not work. However, if the basis of his or her objection is in effect that the treatment is ineffective, then the clinician has an obligation to show why he or she believes this, on the basis of clinical evidence.

Thus, there are moral as well as evidential arguments for changing practice. However, as a matter of health policy, it can be maintained that these arguments should be grounded on common evidential standards, since these standards are public and subject to scientific scrutiny. However, such a line of reasoning is difficult to follow to its end. It seems to be 'utilitarian' in the sense of seeking to maximise total welfare, disregarding the question of whether the trial participants are made better or worse off individually. Competent adult patients are capable of choosing to benefit others at the risk of inflicting harm on themselves; adults with learning disability are arguably not able to do so, and it is very difficult to say whether medical professionals would be able to show that for any given individual it was in his or her best interests to participate in this trial (Edwards 2000: 69, 73).

Notwithstanding the above arguments, if the patients enrolled in the trial are currently not being treated, or being treated unsuccessfully, given that equipoise is attained through the merits of antipsychotic treatment, it is arguable that for these patients randomisation within a placebo-controlled trial is not contrary to their interests. In other words, there is no tension that exists for these individuals between treatment in their best interests, and obtaining scientific evidence about the effectiveness of the treatment under trial (Ashcroft 2000; 320: 1686).

Activity:

Again it is helpful to complete a table of arguments. What are the arguments in favour of conducting a randomised controlled trial (RCT), and which against?

For RCT	Against RCT
For example, the public obligation to evaluate whether the antipsychotic treatment could worsen challenging behaviour	

Prioritise the arguments. Which arguments do you think are most important?

The case study presented here is very complex. Look at the different perspectives and try to complete a total evaluation of the presented case study.

Observe that many themes explored in this workbook are addressed here:

The section on the ethical aspects of the treatment centred on the question about using antipsychotic medication with patients who are not experiencing psychotic symptoms. From a research perspective, there is an obligation to put this type of treatment on a 'better scientific footing'. Various arguments based upon the patient's limited ability to give his or her consent stand against this. (The conflict between research and consent is dealt with in chapter 3.)

People with learning disability are members of a 'vulnerable group'. Is it ethically responsible to run a trial that might help these, or other, vulnerable patients in the future? Or should we limit experiments to direct improvement or healing?

The following article helps us to advance the themes presented in this book through some philosophical considerations.

Philosophical reflections on research with cognitively impaired persons

by Giovanni Maio

Philosophically speaking, any experiment performed on a human subject inevitably brings with it, on the one hand, the reduction of the subject to the status of a thing (as an object of the experiment), and, on the other, an instrumentalisation of that subject, i.e., the person is used for a purpose extraneous to his or her own purposes. If one assumes a basic inviolability and self-purposiveness of any human being, then any experimentation on a human subject is first of all a violation of these fundamental attributes, and therefore can only become morally acceptable through presenting certain grounds of justification. There are two decisive preconditions for the legitimisation of research on human subjects. The first of these is the free and informed consent of the research subject, because, in giving consent the research subject makes the purpose of the experiment into a purpose of his own. Secondly, the therapeutic benefit of the experiment is a prerequisite, because in the instance of a concrete benefit for the research subject, the purpose of the experiment is at least not exclusively a purpose extraneous to the subject. Through this precondition, the instrumentalisation of the research subject is also resolved.

Although both legitimising factors are absent in nontherapeutic research on mentally incapacitated persons, Maio tries, in the following section, to demonstrate that other arguments could justify such research. He considers first the argument of justice. Can the lack of research do harm to the principles of justice? Then

Maio discusses the argument that exclusion of all decisionally-impaired persons from clinical studies would involve a limitation of liberty, i.e., giving expression to their sense of solidarity.

From these initial thoughts it becomes clear why the justification of nontherapeutic research on incapacitated persons is particularly problematic, as, in this situation, both legitimising factors are absent by definition and the question arises as to whether such research is morally justifiable at all. One argument for such nontherapeutic research is the principle of justice as fairness. If one were to renounce all research associated with the diseases afflicting decisionally-impaired persons, then such a renunciation could be understood as a signal that decisionally-impaired persons are not worthy of the scientific endeavour to satisfy their needs. Society is therewith obligated to provide a means for all members of the society to be guaranteed certain basic liberties. Under certain circumstances, an institutionally-decreed global renunciation of any type of research on this group of persons could also be deemed illegitimate. Doing research can carry with it injury to basic personal liberties. Not doing research can also do injury to the principle of justice, because the needs of a particular group may unjustifiably be ignored by the scientific or medical community. This would aggravate the disadvantaged position of this group in a groundless manner and, in particular, would deprive its members of a basis for gaining self-respect.

Maio bases his argument on the principle of justice as fairness. Thus, he raises the second reason for legitimisation of research on human subjects (the prerequisite benefit of the experiment) in a new manner. Mentally-incapacitated persons gain a degree of self-respect through their participation in medical trials, because the researchers performing these trials would be considering them to be normal members of society worthy of advanced medical treatment. Do you regard this as an adequate equivalent? Observe that it does not deal with a therapeutic benefit, in a strict sense.

In the following section, you will see how Maio's first reason for legitimising research on human subjects could be applicable to decisionally-impaired persons.

The principle of justice as fairness points out that a society must search for ways to allow the incapacitated patient to participate in scientific progress in order to provide him or her with the feeling of self-respect. The decisive question is, however, whether every nonbenefit experiment can truly be viewed as a limitation of basic liberties. Does an experiment, which only involves interventions on the level of, for example, obtaining a sample of saliva, also represent an encroachment on basic liberties? The basic liberty of the demented patient would not be injured in the subjection of this person to a negligibly small risk through a study.

Yet, one could argue that the sweeping exclusion of all decisionally-impaired persons from clinical studies would also involve a limitation of liberty because such a categorical exclusion would rob the decisionally-impaired person of the possibility, given a basic altruistic position, of giving expression to her or his sense of solidarity. Only the presumed state of will of the person involved can provide information on the form and extent of a possible infringement of liberty. A study on an incompetent patient is, at the moment of being performed, not an infringement of his basic liberty if one can assume that if one could ask the person, he or she would agree to give consent to participate in the study. The restriction of basic liberty cannot be understood as anything other than an injury to autonomy. The performance of a nonbenefit experiment on a decisionally-impaired person would represent an infringement of the basic liberties even in the presence of the smallest risk imaginable, if the choice of the research subject is based only on the fact that he or she is incapable of defending him or herself.

Experimentation on a decisionally-impaired person can, thus, not be justified if it is performed only because the opportunity happens to be available or because it is the easiest way to gather information. Finally, the ethical legitimacy of instrumentalisation stands and falls with the assessment of whether the research subject in question, if he or she could be asked, would consent to participating. If one could assume that a research subject would consent to a study because, in view of negligible discomfort, he or she would have no reason not to participate, then this study would not represent an infringement of basic liberties. The central argument for limited authorisation of nonbenefit studies on decisionally-impaired persons is the issue of presumed consent and not the postulate of an obligation, no matter how it is justified, to participate in an experiment.

Activity:

Can the requirement of free and informed consent be replaced by presumed consent, i.e., one can presume the consent of a subject in the case of impaired persons?

Maio attempts to demonstrate how research on decisionally-impaired persons could also be legitimate. What is your view? Do you regard both of the named reasons for legitimisation, namely:

1) benefit of gaining self-respect on the basis of the principle of justice as fairness

2) presumed consent

to be sufficient for nontherapeutic research on incapacitated persons?

Consider the following possible objections:

The author argues that, in order to be just, society has to take into account the needs of those people who are not able to fully exercise their right to make decisions. Justice could only be guaranteed by scientific efforts, which include nontherapeutic research. Of course, the patient has certain needs. But his or her first need is not to help possible future patients through scientific research, but rather to get help for him or herself. This would only justify therapeutic research, not nontherapeutic research.

The other argument in the article refers to the presumed state of will of the person. Apart from the difficulties in investigating the state of will of a decisionally-impaired person, it could also be very problematic to expect a sense of solidarity from a person who above all needs our sense of solidarity, and our protection from any danger of abuse.

Think about these, and other, arguments for and against nontherapeutic research on decisionally-impaired persons and form your own opinion.

An open trial of drug X for Alzheimer's disease

by Juan Viñas-Salas and Pekka Louhiala

A proposal for a study of drug X for Alzheimer's disease is presented to the research ethics committee of University Hospital Y in a Southern European country Z. The drug is already commercially available in some countries and the researchers in Y want to participate in a large international study, the aim of which is to evaluate the safety and efficacy of X in patients diagnosed with mild to moderate Alzheimer's disease. Another aim is to give physicians an opportunity to prescribe X for their patients before the official registration of the drug.

The trial lasts twelve weeks and the study subjects are examined several times before, during and after the trial. The endpoints of the study are to measure the quality of life and cognitive status of the patients. These are measured with standardised tests. Informed consent is obtained from the patients.

Activity:

Before you read further, write down the ethical problems that could occur in this case. Imagine the concrete procedure, step by step, and examine the entire set-up and purpose of the trial.

Commentary on ethical issues

First, the issue of informed consent is complicated. While it is probable the patients themselves (at least those with a milder form of disease) can partly understand what the study is about, they cannot give their consent in the same sense as competent adults can. Therefore, their relatives should somehow be involved in the process. Here is an obvious analogy with the situation in research involving children. In neither case should the capacity for informed consent be treated as an all-or-nothing phenomenon.

Second, since a widely accepted standard treatment for Alzheimer's disease does not exist, there may be pressure from family members to have patients enrolled in the study. The role conflict between a physician and a researcher is obviously an ethical problem here also. If the physician is convinced of the usefulness of X, it may be difficult for him or her to give neutral information of the study to potential study subjects and their relatives.

Activity:

If you wish to reacquaint yourself with the problem of the role conflict between physician and researcher, return to the article *The conceptual foundations of scientific research and medical practice*, p. 9 of this volume.

Although X is licensed in some countries, the need for large international studies demonstrates that the position of X in the treatment of Alzheimer's disease is not settled and that X may even turn out to be harmful for the patients.

Third, an element of marketing plays a role in this kind of research. If the drug is finally licensed, physicians have already developed the habit of prescribing it.

Fourth, it is not clear that international studies, in which measuring the quality of life of patients is one endpoint, are even possible. For the validity of the study, the tests performed should be identical, but due to cultural differences the concepts of high or low quality of life are probably understood differently, depending on the culture. This is especially obvious if tests developed within the Anglo-American culture are applied in a Mediterranean country.

Fifth, the relevance of the whole study should be considered carefully. If X is already licensed in some countries, why is there a need for this particular study? If we still lack conclusive information about the safety and efficacy of X, has licensing taken place prematurely in those countries?

The fact that the research is part of an international study places a high expectation on the researcher to be diligent. The fact that X is already licensed in some countries obliges researchers to consider the experimental results, which already exist. This issue will be further explored in the next chapter.

– 5 –

The extent of the researcher's duties

In the previous three chapters we have been considering how ethically to regulate research involving human subjects. Accordingly, we have focused on the responsibility of the researcher towards subjects. We have considered, for example, whether, and to what extent, property rights and inducements in medical research should be regulated (chapter 2), whether paternalism with regard to the subject is ethically necessary (chapter 3), and we have discussed the particular ethical issues which arise when undertaking medical research on vulnerable groups (chapters 3 and 4).

In this last chapter, we will now take much more into account the responsibility of the researcher towards his or her sponsor and towards the scientific community. After examining the case and commentaries of the open label extension study, we will consider the relationship between 'bad science' and 'bad ethics'.

The case of the open label extension study

by Paul Wainwright

Case study

The following case study illustrates a situation in which the possibility of a proper consent becomes a central issue. In particular it raises questions about the extent to which the convenience of the researcher (and possibly, by extension, the concerns of society) can justifiably override the concerns of the individual research subject.

The example concerns open label extension studies to evaluate the safety and efficacy of investigational drugs, say, for the sake of illustration, a drug intended for the management of chronic pain from a neuropathy. In this design patients who have previously been enrolled in a Phase III randomised double-blind placebo-controlled trial are asked to consent to a further period of study for one year, during which they know that they will all receive the study drug.[6] The patients will know they have been in a trial of the new drug but they will not know which arm of the Phase III trial they were in or whether they were taking the investigational drug or a placebo. If they enter the extension study they may therefore either be continuing to take the study drug or they may start taking it for the first time, following a period on placebo. The investigators argue that it is not desirable or possible to unblind the patient's allocation in the first study prior to their consent for the extension study because this would jeopardise the double-blind design.

In the following two commentaries, the authors examine different aspects of the case. At first, P. Wainwright discusses the different options presented to a patient who is considering entering the extension study. This leads to the question of how appropriate is it to recruit a person who might not require medication. The second aspect in his commentary refers to the question of whether there is scientific merit in not unblinding subjects prior to their enrolment in the open label study.

In the second commentary, S. Lötjönen considers the question of whether the trial is badly designed if the concealment of allocation of patients is maintained. Further, she takes up the theme of a patient's safety and autonomy. Finally, she describes possible motives for why the investigators should maintain concealment.

6 This research method is relatively common. A recent MEDLINE search for 'open label extension studies," limited by publication type to randomised controlled trials, produced 55 references between 1992 and 2000.

Commentaries on the case

Commentary

by Paul Wainwright

The case raises several questions. Clearly it is important to maintain the concealment of allocation of patients in the Phase III trial until after the data have been analysed, for all the same reasons that the double-blind randomised control trial design was adopted in the first place. It is, of course, possible to break the code for any participant at any time, in the event of an emergency or an adverse event. If this were to happen, the problems alluded to above, of unblinding and the consequent risk of bias, will apply.

Patients are recruited to trials and commence treatment one by one, over a period of several weeks or months, and each will thus have different start and completion dates. They will therefore also approach the open-label extension study one by one. Thus the dangers of unblinding will apply until the last subject from a centre completes the Phase III trial. But each patient, one by one, must decide whether or not to enter the extension study at the point at which she or he completes her or his involvement in the Phase III trial. The requirement for a valid consent is that the subject is in possession of, and understands, all relevant information. The one piece of information the subject will not be given–must not be given, if one accepts the arguments of the investigators–is whether she or he has been taking active medication during the Phase III trial or whether she or he has been taking placebo.

However, it could be argued that this is the one piece of information, over and above what the subject will already know from the previous trial information sheet, that is relevant and necessary for a proper consent. Consider the options:

1. The subject was receiving active medication
2. The subject was receiving placebo

A. The subject received good relief of symptoms with minimal side effects

B. The subject did not receive good relief of symptoms and/or had unpleasant side effects

These can, of course, be combined as 1A, 1B, 2A, or 2B.

Activity:

Imagine yourself in the situation of the research subject, who is asked to participate in the following extension study. If you could find out which of the four groups (1A, 1B, 2A, 2B) you belonged to, in which group(s) would you consent to join the extension study and in which group(s) would you refuse? However, as you do not know if 1 or 2 applies to you, in which situation would you have the greatest difficulty coming to a decision, and why?

But observe that A and B are theoretical options and 'real life patients' often fall between the groups, e.g., the subject received good relief from symptoms with minimal but unpleasant side effects.

For subjects considering entering the extension study, it would clearly seem to be in their interests to know in which of these categories they fall. If a subject was in 1A, taking an active drug and getting good pain relief, she or he is likely to wish to enter the extension study. If a subject experienced 1B, taking an active drug with poor relief, it would be in her or his interests to leave the trial and try one of the other medications available to treat this condition. Subjects who fall into 2A are in an interesting position. They have achieved good symptom relief without active medication, either through the power of placebo or because they are in spontaneous remission. Is it appropriate to recruit someone who may have no need of medication and start her or him on a year's course of an experimental drug? Not knowing they were taking placebo and finding their symptoms relieved, these subjects might enter the extension study in the belief that they must have in fact been in 1A and this is their best option for continued symptom relief. Subjects in 2B have a straight gamble: if they think they were taking active medication, they will refuse the extension study, but if they think they must have been taking placebo they might well decide to enter the study in the hope that the active drug will work for them.

When trial subjects are first recruited to randomised-controlled trials they are told about the randomisation process, often with reference to the example of tossing a coin. It is made quite clear that chance is at work and no one can know which arm of the trial he or she will enter. This element of chance is a necessary component of the trial method and is justified in the interests of good science. However, when the study becomes an open label one it is difficult to see any justification, in the context of the new study, for keeping up the concealment.

It might be argued that there is scientific merit in not unblinding subjects prior to their enrolment in the open label study. In an ideal trial one might imagine, at the end of the double-blind comparison phase, those subjects who received active treatment showing sound improvement in their condition. Those receiving placebo would show little or no improvement. At the end of the open label extension phase, the subjects in the active treatment group would continue to show good results, and those in the placebo group would also achieve good results, comparable to those who had been receiving active treatment all along. The open label phase, following the double-blind phase in this way, and maintaining the concealment of which arm of the trial the patient had been in, would thus add useful weight to the evidence for the therapeutic benefit of the new drug. A psychological benefit would thus be minimised which could otherwise develop if the patient were told that he or she was in the placebo group and would now be receiving the real medication. Limiting the knowledge of the patient protects the integrity of the trial's findings.

Activity:

How do you evaluate the argument mentioned above for continuing the concealment? Do you find it convincing? What do you think about the argument that if the results of the double-blind comparison phase are given, then a huge selection bias would develop in the open label phase?

However, this would seem to suggest a marked lack of confidence in the randomised controlled trial as a research design. The whole point of such an experiment is to argue that the experimental drug has a therapeutic benefit that exceeds the effect of a placebo. At the end of the double-blind phase we should have the data that tell us how effective the drug might be and if the randomised controlled trial design is sufficiently suited to its purpose. If the results are inconclusive, it would seem to suggest we need to do further controlled experiments. If the results are positive, then we should have confidence in them and act accordingly.

Comparative analysis of the placebo and active treatment groups at the end of the open label study sounds suspiciously like superstition, metaphorically crossing our fingers in the hope that the results will turn out right.

A further commentary is presented in the following paper, which introduces additional ethical issues with respect to the case examined above.

Commentary

by Salla Lötjönen

Trial design

A trial that is badly designed and cannot answer the questions it seeks to answer is considered futile and therefore exposes the participants to unnecessary risks and burdens. A badly designed trial is therefore unethical. A good trial design is based on all obtainable previous knowledge on the safety and efficacy of the investigational drug and is designed in a way that is able to meet the criteria that medical science has set for scientific validity.

Activity:

In this commentary Lötjönen calls attention to one of the central obligations of a researcher: the collection of all obtainable previous knowledge on the safety and efficacy of the investigational drug. This obligation results not only from the effort to create as successful a trial design as possible, but also from the researcher's duty to protect the research subjects.

But is a badly designed trial unethical in every case? Are there any counter examples? Does this view tend to reduce the ethical questions to technical ones of trial design?

Here, the investigators argue that they cannot break the code of randomisation until the participant has consented to take part in the trial, as this would jeopardise the double-blind design. However, the previous study and the study in concern are clearly different studies with different goals. According to the principles of good trial design, and in order to begin a new trial on the same substance, it would not only be advisable but also necessary to analyse the results of the previous study to know whether the second trial is worthwhile at all and to know on which basis the next study should be built.

Patient safety

Not only does this case raise issues concerning the ethics of trial design, but it also takes up the question of patient safety. If the previous study demonstrates, once analysed, that the patients did not benefit from the substance and that, in addition to the drug being ineffective, it had some unpleasant side effects, the new study will then cause unnecessary danger to the health of the participants. This trial clearly does not meet any of the ethical criteria, as now the trial is not only futile, but is also harmful to the subjects that take part in it.

Patient autonomy

Even if the two previously mentioned aspects could be circumvented by revealing some details of the case that do not appear in the case description, the question about patient autonomy still remains. A necessary condition to informed consent is that the patients know what they are subjecting themselves to. The investigators have a duty to find out all relevant information obtainable already prior to the start of the study and they also have a duty to reveal it to the subjects.

All details of the research protocol are naturally not interesting to the subjects, but one can say that knowing whether the subject received placebo or the active medication lies at the core of the matter when the subject is asked to decide whether to enrol in the next step. As the information would, objectively (and depending on the individual, subjectively) speaking, be relevant to patient choice, the blinding should be uncovered and the information given not only to the investigators, but also to the participants.

Activity:

Lötjönen points out that in this case fundamental ethical criteria are not met. As the investigators refuse to utilise all available knowledge about the investigational drug,

a) they endanger the safety of the patients, and

b) they restrict the autonomy of the subjects.

But the investigators could present some objections to this analysis. They do not endanger the safety of the patients at all, because in the previous study no, or only minimal, side effects in any patient could be observed. Thus, the new study will not cause any danger to the health of the participants. And the investigators would not restrict the autonomy of the patients, because they, the patients, are absolutely free to refuse to participate in the new study.

What is your view?

Possible real motives for the investigators

What then would be the real motive for the investigators not to disclose to participants to which study group they belonged and to recruit them to the next trial already at this stage? One very likely reason is that the investigators fear losing contact with the subjects, and maintaining contact with them would save the investigators a lot of time and effort if they could receive informed consent from the participants at their last visit to the previous trial instead of having to contact them at a later stage. It may also be that they fear losing participants to the new trial who already know how they were grouped and what they received in each group during the treatment. As mentioned previously, the participants who did not gain good symptom relief from the drug, or the ones who did not really need the drug, do not have an objective interest to take part in the trial, which could make it harder for the investigators to get a sufficient number of participants to enrol in the study.

In addition, financial interests play an important role in trials on pharmaceuticals. The pharmaceutical industry makes huge investments in developing new products, and the quicker they can get the products out on the market, the sooner they will start earning back the investments made. Initiating the next phase already before the previous one has ended would save the industry a considerable amount of time. Additionally, if the investigators would have to start finding more recruits after half of the original participants had refused to continue in the trial, the completion of the study would again be delayed. However, lack of time or pressure from the sponsor does not relieve the investigators from their duties 1) to conduct good quality research, 2) to safeguard the safety of the patients or 3) to ensure that the patients have given consent that is based on sufficient knowledge.

Activity:

One could argue that the researchers restrict the patient's autonomy in the trial design because of the pressure they are under from the sponsor; thus, the autonomy of the investigators is also limited. However, one must ask if the situation of the researcher and the patient is comparable, or whether a researcher has by definition more autonomy than a patient who is suffering from a disease; additionally, it is the researcher who is responsible for the trial design and not the patient.

Consider what disadvantages could ensue for the investigators if they were to resist the pressures of the sponsor? Take into account the marketing interests of the sponsor.

In the next case study, we will consider the ethical relevance of scientific quality. The discussion returns us to the issue of the relationship between scientific research and medical practice (chapter 1, p. 9) and addresses the fundamental problem in research ethics, namely, the tension between researcher and physician.

Bad science–bad ethics?

by Pekka Louhiala

A randomised placebo-controlled trial was conducted to investigate the effect of dietary magnesium on mild to moderate hypertension. The design of the study was a crossover trial and the total number of subjects in the study was seventeen. The results were published in the British Medical Journal

(BMJ) and the conclusion was: 'The results provide no evidence for a role of dietary magnesium in the regulation of high blood pressure.'

Activity:

Assume that you are a member of a research ethics committee evaluating a protocol proposing the above trial. Assume further that the process of obtaining the informed consent of study subjects is satisfactory. Do you find any ethical problems in the design?

The study was conducted and published in the mid-1980s and the world of scientific review of research has changed since then. It is less probable that the study would be published in the BMJ today, even if the debate on the effect of dietary magnesium were still open. The main reason for this is the inadequate *power* of the design to detect even moderate differences between dietary magnesium and placebo. Due to the small number of patients in the study, the results of the study remain inconclusive.

This is just an example of the numerous issues inherent in any discussion on the design of clinical trials, issues that not only call into question the scientific validity of a design but also raise highly important ethical issues. Already the Nuremberg code (→ Appendix 1, p.108) asserts that 'The experiment should be such as to yield fruitful results for the good of society' (No.2). This can easily be interpreted to imply a requirement for a sound design of studies. If it is probable that a study design does not yield results that either support or refute the proposed hypothesis, then it would be better not to begin the project at all.

Too small a sample size is perhaps the most common dilemma that researchers face. Many of the therapies discarded as ineffective after inconclusive 'negative' trials may still have a clinically meaningful effect. There is not a simple solution to the question of sample size. Increasing size presents more reliable results but also increases the expense of a study. The researchers have to find a balance between the two. Yet, too large a sample size may also be unethical in the sense that resources are wasted, and reliable conclusions could have been drawn using a smaller group of research subjects.

Issues that are both scientific and ethical arise in every phase of a study from the initial stages of planning it to publishing the results of it. Errors in data collection, data processing or data analysis distort the results and may lead to unjustified changes in practice. Also, the presentation, interpretation and publication of the results are phases in which various biases may endanger the scientific and ethical soundness of the research in question. Examples of the biases in the later phases are *publication bias* (disappointed scientists do not publish negative results) and *abstracting bias* (the abstract of the article exaggerates the results). The importance of a publication bias is acknowledged also in the latest version of the Helsinki Declaration (→Appendix 3, p.123), which states that 'Negative as well as positive results should be published or otherwise publicly available' (B. 27).

While it is widely agreed that bad science is bad ethics, uniform procedures do not exist to evaluate this side of research. The research ethics committees may have a role in the evaluation of a study's scientific validity, but in many cases the members of these committees lack adequate expertise. Perhaps ethics committees should maintain a network of experts available in cases where the expertise of individual members is not enough to evaluate the different aspects of a study.

Activity:

In the paper above, reference is made to the importance of publishing negative results of research. Why is this so difficult? Could this be in part due to disappointment in the results, but more importantly due to the role conflict between physician and researcher, which is described at the beginning of this book?

It is stated above that 'scientific knowledge is not the aim of medical practice, but rather a *means* to perform effectively medicine's central task of promoting or restoring health' (p.12).

Therefore, if research yields negative results, then the researcher does not seem to be effectively performing medicine's central task, that of promoting or restoring health. We have reached the end of the book, and again we are considering the tension between researcher and physician; indeed, at this point in the discussion, the tension might be at its greatest. However, in order to further the primary goal of medicine, it is important that negative results are published. Negative outcomes of research can be as important as positive ones.

As your final activity we would like you to review some of the earlier activities and see whether some of your responses have changed.

Try to draw up a case where you think that the conflict between medical practice and scientific research is so great that scientific research should not be allowed (see p. 14).

Is the participation in risky, nontherapeutic experiments a choice that the potential subject should not be asked to make (see p. 30)?

What do you think about a physician-researcher who is claiming: 'I act ethically correctly, because I comply with all the regulations' (see p. 55)?

Think about the arguments for and against nontherapeutic research on decisionally-impaired persons and form your own opinion (see p. 84).

Glossary

Autonomy Term originating from the Greek *autos* (self) and *nomos* (rule or law) and meaning self-determination or self-rule. In some theories of biomedical ethics, respect for autonomy is the most important consideration. Discussions of autonomy focus on the necessary and sufficient conditions needed for autonomy.

In bioethics, the principle of autonomy primarily refers to the obligation of healthcare professionals to respect the right of patients to make their own decisions concerning treatment. Constraints on autonomy could be in the form of coercion and undue influence. Other constraints arise within the individual, who is, for example, not capable of making decisions for her or himself.

Bias A research study is generally open to a number of potential errors. Bias denotes a systematic error. Sources of bias are, for example, the assignment of comparison groups or unequal interventions in a trial.

Blinding There are two kinds of blinding. In a single-blind design the assignment of agents or procedures being tested are not known to the patients; in a double-blind design these assignments are not known to either the examining health care professionals or to the patients.

Cohort study In this type of study a group or groups of individuals are defined on the basis of presence or absence of exposure to a suspected risk factor or on the basis of being treated or not. The group is then followed for a certain period of time. In an 'experimental study' the difference between the comparison groups is intentionally introduced by the investigators.

Crossover study Both groups in a study receive both treatments but in the reverse order.

Cross-sectional study The term refers to the interval of data collection, or, the period of time during which data are collected. The study is 'cross-sectional' if the researcher wishes to collect information at one point in time. The study is 'longitudinal' if the researcher is studying one or more populations over a period of time.

Deontological The word deontological comes from the Greek *deon*, meaning 'duty' or 'binding'. Deontological ethics try to identify and justify duties that are binding for an individual and more or less independent of the practical concerns facing that individual.

Equipoise Research trial equipoise is the state before carrying out a clinical study in which the community of expert clinicians is undecided as to the preferred treatment for the given population, as determined by the study's eligibility criteria. The study should be designed to disturb clinical equipoise and to terminate when a better treatment has been found.

Haemorrhage Bleeding.

Historical controls Type of control used in a case-control study, such as, for example, when the researcher uses knowledge about earlier untreated individuals as a comparison with present clinical subjects being treated with the new regime.

Informed consent 'In any research on human beings, each potential subject must be adequately informed of the aims, methods, sources of funding, any possible conflicts of interest, institutional affiliations of the researcher, the anticipated benefits and potential risks of the study and the discomfort it may entail. The subject should be informed of the right to abstain from participation in the study or to withdraw consent to participate at any time without reprisal. After ensuring that the subject has understood the information, the physician should then obtain the subject's freely-given informed consent, preferably in writing. If the consent cannot be obtained in writing, the non-written consent must be formally documented and witnessed' (Helsinki Declaration B.22).

Justice The term means 'law' or 'lawfulness', but is used in a broader sense to mean 'fairness'. The distribution of something can be based on different principles of justice: arithmetical equality, merit (or deserts) or need.

Kant The ideas concerning morality explored by the German philosopher Immanuel Kant (1724–1804) are widely influential in ethical discussion. Respect for persons is a basic idea of Kantian ethics and includes the requirement that we regard each person as possessing inherent dignity and infinite worth. We should never treat other people as mere means to an end, but, rather as an end in themselves.

Locke The ideas of the English philosopher John Locke (1632–1704) are widely influential in the philosophical and bioethical discussion about personhood. He differentiates between the idea of 'Man' and that of 'Person'. A man's identity is grounded in a living body, in the participation of the same continued life. But a person's identity is that of a thinking intelligent being.

Open label extension study A study of a drug which takes place on completion of a randomised controlled trial and initiated to gather further data about safety, efficacy, tolerability, etc. In the open-label extension study all those who consent to take part knowingly (openly) receive the investigational drug.

Paternalism A term used to describe the theory of overriding the decisions of a person with the intention of benefiting that person.

Perioperative A term denoting the period of time during an operation.

Phase I, II, III and IV These indicators signify different phases in drug development. They give the clinical research its structure. Phase I trials often involve healthy subjects and examine the pharmacokinetics (which include absorption, distribution, metabolism and excretion) and toxicity of new drugs. Phase II inquiries test for preliminary efficacy of a drug or a procedure. Phase II investigation may involve randomised controls, whereas phase III investigation is almost always a 'randomised controlled trial'. The efficacy and safety of a trial are compared with those of another therapy. Phase IV trials are postmarketing trials, performed when the medical product has a marketing authorisation. The effectiveness is examined in Phase IV trials.

Placebo An inert substance, often used in randomised controlled trials as a control treatment in comparison to an experimental treatment, if no standard treatment exists.

Proxy consent In the case of a minor or a decisionally-impaired adult, a legal guardian or representative can decide on his or her behalf. In the case of a minor, the parents or a local authority are the legal guardians. In the case of an adult, legal representation has been settled differently in various jurisdictions.

Randomised controlled trial (RCT) This form of investigation involves one or more treatment groups and a control group that will typically receive a placebo or the standard therapy. The goal of randomisation (a simple random method is flipping a coin) is to combat bias in group assignments. The larger the groups, the more likely that randomisation will produce similar groups.

Risk-benefit assessment 'Every medical research project involving human subjects should be preceded by careful assessment of predictable risks and burdens in comparison with foreseeable benefits to the subject or others' (Helsinki Declaration B.16). The assessment is to take into account that risks or burdens, such as hair loss, inconvenience, or extra costs, may be more important from the perspective of one patient, but not of another patient or of the investigator.

Sepsis Infection of the blood.

Splenectomy Excision or extirpation of the spleen. Excision means partial, extirpation means complete removal of an organ.

Standard therapy The therapy used for a disorder in question that is recommended according to established scientific knowledge. It is used as a control treatment to act as a means of comparison by which the experimental treatment is evaluated. If no standard treatment exists, a placebo is used.

Teratogen Anything capable of disrupting foetal growth and producing malformation. It can be classified as drugs, poisons, radiation, physical agents.

Utilitarianism The concept names an extended family of ethical theories. These theories hold that good results are results that maximise benefits and minimise harm. In its classical form (J. S. Mill) 'actions are right in proportion as they tend to promote happiness, wrong as they tend to produce the reverse of happiness'.

Vulnerable groups Two groups of people are most often considered vulnerable research subjects: 1) people who are incapable of giving informed consent, and 2) people who are likely to be coerced or manipulated. The first group represents children and persons who are impaired by mental illness or retardation. The second group represents institutionalised persons such as prisoners, or hospital staff and persons who are in a special situation such as women who are pregnant or individuals facing a crisis, such as those suffering from depression. Fear, ignorance or pressure can account for their agreement to participate in research. Enrolling vulnerable research subjects in research protocols often requires special justification.

'Wash-out' period The time period during which the effect of treatment disappears. In clinical trials fashioned after the crossover design, the term is used to avoid 'carry-over' effects (effects of the first treatment being carried over into the second period).

References

Angell, M. 2000. The pharmaceutical industry–to whom is it accountable? *New England Journal of Medicine* 342: 1902–04.

Anonymous. 2000. Safeguarding participants in clinical trials. Editorial. *The Lancet* 355 (9222): 2177.

Ashcroft, R. E. 1999. Equipoise, knowledge and ethics in clinical research and practice. *Bioethics* 13: 314–26.

Ashcroft, R. E. 2000. Giving medicine a fair trial. *British Medical Journal* 320: 1686.

Ashcroft, R., B. Fraser, M. Kerr and Z. Ahmed 2001. Are antipsychotic drugs the right treatment for challenging behaviour in learning disability: The place of a randomised trial. *Journal of Medical Ethics* 27: 338–43.

Baum, M. 2000. Declaration of Helsinki should be strengthened: Against. *British Medical Journal* 321: 444–45.

Bauman, Z. 1993. *Postmodern ethics*. Oxford: Blackwell.

Bedau, H. A. 1995. Paternalism. In: Honderich, T. (ed.), *The Oxford Companion to Philosophy*, p. 647. Oxford: Oxford University Press.

Britton, A., M. McKee, N. Black, K. McPherson, C. Sanderson and C. Bain 1998. Choosing between randomised and non-randomised studies: a systematic review. *Health Technology Assessment* 2: i-iv, 1–124.

Chadwick, R. 2000. Informed consent in genetic research. In: Doyal, L. and J. Tobias (eds), *Informed Consent in Medical Research*, p. 203–10. London: BMJBooks.

Council of Europe Recommendation No. R (90) 3 of the Committee of Ministers to member states concerning medical research on human beings.

Cullinan, T. 1997. Informed consent: Other societies have different concepts of autonomy. *British Medical Journal* 315: 248.

Dickenson, D. 1997. *Property, women and politics*. Cambridge: Polity Press.

Downie, R. S., and K. C. Calman 1987. *Healthy respect: Ethics in health care*. London: Faber.

Edwards, S. D. 2000. An argument against research on people with intellectual disabilities. *Medicine, Health Care and Philosophy* 3: 69–73.

Emerson, E. and J. Bromley 1995. The form and function of challenging behaviours. *Journal of Intellectual Disability Research* 39: 388–98.

Evans, D. and M. Evans 1996. *A Decent Proposal – Ethical Review of Clinical Research*. Chichester: Wiley.

Explanatory Report to the Convention for the Protection of Human Rights and Dignity of the Human Being with Regard to the Application of Biology and Medicine: Convention on Human Rights and Biomedicine, Directorate of Legal Affairs, Strasbourg, May 1997. DIR/JUR 5.

Food and Drug Administration 1977. General Considerations for the Clinical Evaluation of Drugs. HEW Publication No. (FDA) 77-3040.

Food and Drug Administration 1997. 62:185 Title 21 CFR [= Code of Federal Regulations] Part 312 Docket No. 97N-0030

Gold, R. E. 1996. *Body parts: Property rights and the ownership of human biological materials*. Washington: Georgetown University Press.

Hanson, M. J. and D. Callahan 1999. *The goals of medicine: The forgotten issue in health care reform*. Washington: Georgetown University Press.

Hansson, M. 1998. Balancing the quality of consent. *Journal of Medical Ethics* 24: 182–87.

Hewlett, S. 1996. Consent to clinical research. *Journal of Medical Ethics* 22: 232–37.

Höfling, W. and M. Demel 1999. Zur Forschung an Nichteinwilligungsfähigen. *Medizinrecht* **12**: 540–546.

International Conference on Harmonisation Good Clinical Practice Guidelines. Committee for Proprietary Medicinal Products (CPMP) of the European Agency for the Evaluation of Medicinal Products (EMEA) 135/95.

Kant, I. 1988 (reprint). *Fundamental Principles of the Metaphysic of Morals*. Amherst, New York: Prometheus Books.

Macklin, R. 1999. The ethical problems with sham surgery in clinical research. *New England Journal of Medicine* 341: 992–96.

Maio, G. 2001. Zur Begründung einer Ethik der Forschung an nicht einwilligungsfähigen Patienten. *Zeitschrift für Evangelische Ethik* 45: 135–48.

Marckmann, G. 2001. Teaching science vs. the apprentice model–do we really have the choice? *Medicine, Health Care and Philosophy* 4: 85–89.

Marx, K. 1973 (reprint). *Grundrisse*. Harmondsworth: Penguin.

Medical Research Council 1991. The ethical conduct of research on the mentally incapacitated. London: Medical Research Council.

Medical Research Council 1998. Guidelines for good clinical practice in clinical trials. London: Medical Research Council.

Medical research involving incapacitated persons. Report to the Minister of Health, Welfare and Sport and the Minister of Justice regarding the regulation of medical research involving minors and incapacitated persons. Rijswijk, the Netherlands, 16 May 1995, section 7, subsection 7.2.

Mental Health Act 1983. London: HMSO.

Montgomery, J. 1997. *Health Care Law*. Oxford: Oxford University Press.

Munson, R. 1981. Why medicine cannot be a science. *The Journal of Medicine and Philosophy* 6: 183–208.

Nuffield Council on Bioethics 2000. Stem Cell Therapy: the ethical issues. A discussion paper. London: Nuffield Council on Bioethics.

Office for Protection from Research Risks [OPRR] Reports Number 93–4 [Human Subject Protections] 1993.

Pellegrino, E. D. 1999. The goals and ends of medicine: How are they to be defined? In: Hanson, M. J. and D. Callahan (eds), *The goals of medicine: The forgotten issue in health care reform*, p. 55–68. Washington: Georgetown University Press.

Re C (adult: refusal of medical treatment) [1994] 1 All ER [= All England Law Reports] 819.

Rothman, K. J. and K. B. Michels 1994. The continuing unethical use of placebo controls. *New England Journal of Medicine* 331: 394–98.

Rothman, K. J. and K. B. Michels 2000. Declaration of Helsinki should be strengthened: For. *British Medical Journal* 321: 442–44.

Rynning, E. 2001. The Regulation of Neonatal Research in Sweden. In: Mason, S. and C. Megone (eds), *European Neonatal Research – Consent, Ethics Committees and Law*, p.167–183, Aldershot: Ashgate.

Schüklenk, U. 2000. Protecting the vulnerable: Testing times for clinical research ethics. *Social Science and Medicine* 51: 969–77.

Tobias, J. S. 1997. BMJ's present policy (sometimes approving research in which patients have not given fully informed consent) is wholly correct. *British Medical Journal* 314: 1111–14.

Toellner, R. 1990. Problemgeschichte: Entstehung der Ethik-Kommissionen. In: Toellner, R., (ed.), *Die Ethik-Kommission in der Medizin. Problemgeschichte, Aufgabenstellung, Arbeitsweise, Rechtsstellung und Organisationsformen Medizinischer Ethik-Kommissionen*, p. 3–18. Stuttgart, New York: Gustav Fischer.

Waldron, J. 1988. *The right to private property*. Oxford: Clarendon Press.

Weijer, C. 1999. Placebo-controlled trials in schizophrenia: Are they ethical? Are they necessary? *Schizophrenia Research* 35: 211–18.

Wieland, W. 1975. *Diagnose. Überlegungen zur Medizintheorie.* Berlin, New York: Walter de Gruyter.

Wiesing, U. 1993. Medizin zwischen Wissenschaft, Technologie und Kunst. *Zeitschrift für Medizinische Ethik* 39: 121–30.

Appendices

(1) The Nuremberg Code

From 'Trials of War Criminals Before the Nuremberg Military Tribunals Under Control Council Law No. 10', Vol. 2, Nuremberg, October 1946 – April 1949. (Washington, DC: US Government Printing Office, 1949). pp 181–182.

The great weight of the evidence before us is to the effect that certain types of medical experiments on human beings, when kept within reasonably well-defined bounds, conform to the ethics of the medical profession generally. The protagonists of the practice of human experimentation justify their views on the basis that such experiments yield results for the good of society that are unprocurable by other methods or means of study. All agree, however, that certain basic principles must be observed in order to satisfy moral, ethical and legal concepts.

1. The voluntary consent of the human subject is absolutely essential. This means that the person involved should have legal capacity to give consent; should be so situated as to be able to exercise free power of choice, without the intervention of any element of force, fraud, deceit, duress, overreaching, or other ulterior form of constraint or coercion; and should have sufficient knowledge and comprehension of the elements of the subject matter involved as to enable him to make an understanding and enlightened decision. This latter element requires that

before the acceptance of an affirmative decision by the experimental subject there should be made known to him the nature, duration, and purpose of the experiment; the method and means by which it is to be conducted; all inconveniences and hazards reasonably to be expected; and the effects upon his health or person which may possibly come from his participation in the experiment. The duty and responsibility for ascertaining the quality of the consent rests upon each individual who initiates, directs or engages in the experiment. It is a personal duty and responsibility which may not be delegated to another with impunity.

2. The experiment should be such as to yield fruitful results for the good of society, unprocurable by other methods or means of study, and not random and unnecessary in nature.
3. The experiment should be so designed and based on the results of animal experimentation and a knowledge of the natural history of the disease or other problems under study that the anticipated results will justify the performance of the experiment.
4. The experiment should be so conducted as to avoid all unnecessary physical and mental suffering and injury.
5. No experiment should be conducted where there is an a priori reason to believe that death or disabling injury will occur; except perhaps, in those experiments where the experimental physicians also serve as subjects.
6. The degree of risk to be taken should never exceed that determined by the humanitarian importance of the problem to be solved by the experiment.
7. Proper preparations should be made and adequate facilities provided to protect the experimental subject against even remote possibilities of injury, disability, or death.
8. The experiment should be conducted only by scientifically qualified persons. The highest degree of skill and care should be required through all stages of the experiment of those who conduct or engage in the experiment.
9. During the course of the experiment the human subject should be at liberty to bring the experiment to an end if he has reached the physical or mental state where continuation of the experiment seems to him to be impossible.

10. During the course of the experiment the scientist in charge must be prepared to terminate the experiment at any stage, if he has probable cause to believe in the exercise of the good faith, superior skill and careful judgement required of him that a continuation of the experiment is likely to result in injury, disability, or death to the experimental subject.

(2) Council of Europe Convention on Human Rights and Biomedicine

Convention for the protection of Human Rights and Dignity of the Human Being with regard to the application of Biology and Medicine: Convention on Human Rights and Biomedicine (Oviedo, 4.IV.1997)

Preamble

The member States of the Council of Europe, the other States and the European Community, signatories hereto,

Bearing in mind the Universal Declaration of Human Rights proclaimed by the General Assembly of the United Nations on 10 December 1948;

Bearing in mind the Convention for the Protection of Human Rights and Fundamental Freedoms of 4 November 1950;

Bearing in mind the European Social Charter of 18 October 1961;

Bearing in mind the International Covenant on Civil and Political Rights and the International Covenant on Economic, Social and Cultural Rights of 16 December 1966;

Bearing in mind the Convention for the Protection of Individuals with regard to Automatic Processing of Personal Data of 28 January 1981;

Bearing also in mind the Convention on the Rights of the Child of 20 November 1989;

Considering that the aim of the Council of Europe is the achievement of a greater unity between its members and that one of the methods by which that aim is to be pursued is the maintenance and further realisation of human rights and fundamental freedoms;

Conscious of the accelerating developments in biology and medicine;

Convinced of the need to respect the human being both as an individual and as a member of the human species and recognising the importance of ensuring the dignity of the human being;

Conscious that the misuse of biology and medicine may lead to acts endangering human dignity;

Affirming that progress in biology and medicine should be used for the benefit of present and future generations;

Stressing the need for international cooperation so that all humanity may enjoy the benefits of biology and medicine;

Recognising the importance of promoting a public debate on the questions posed by the application of biology and medicine and the responses to be given thereto;

Wishing to remind all members of society of their rights and responsibilities;

Taking account of the work of the Parliamentary Assembly in this field, including Recommendation 1160 (1991) on the preparation of a convention on bioethics;

Resolving to take such measures as are necessary to safeguard human dignity and the fundamental rights and freedoms of the individual with regard to the application of biology and medicine,

Have agreed as follows:

Chapter I – General provisions

Article 1 – Purpose and object

Parties to this Convention shall protect the dignity and identity of all human beings and guarantee everyone, without discrimination, respect for their integrity and other rights and fundamental freedoms with regard to the application of biology and medicine.

Each Party shall take in its internal law the necessary measures to give effect to the provisions of this Convention.

Article 2 – Primacy of the human being

The interests and welfare of the human being shall prevail over the sole interest of society or science.

Article 3 – Equitable access to health care
Parties, taking into account health needs and available resources, shall take appropriate measures with a view to providing, within their jurisdiction, equitable access to health care of appropriate quality.

Article 4 – Professional standards
Any intervention in the health field, including research, must be carried out in accordance with relevant professional obligations and standards.

Chapter II – Consent

Article 5 – General rule
An intervention in the health field may only be carried out after the person concerned has given free and informed consent to it.

This person shall beforehand be given appropriate information as to the purpose and nature of the intervention as well as on its consequences and risks.

The person concerned may freely withdraw consent at any time.

Article 6 – Protection of persons not able to consent

1 Subject to Articles 17 and 20 below, an intervention may only be carried out on a person who does not have the capacity to consent, for his or her direct benefit.

2 Where, according to law, a minor does not have the capacity to consent to an intervention, the intervention may only be carried out with the authorisation of his or her representative or an authority or a person or body provided for by law.

   The opinion of the minor shall be taken into consideration as an increasingly determining factor in proportion to his or her age and degree of maturity.

3 Where, according to law, an adult does not have the capacity to consent to an intervention because of a mental disability, a disease or for similar reasons, the intervention may only be carried out with the authorisation of his or her representative or an authority or a person or body provided for by law.

   The individual concerned shall as far as possible take part in the authorisation procedure.

4 The representative, the authority, the person or the body mentioned in paragraphs 2 and 3 above shall be given, under the same conditions, the information referred to in Article 5.
5 The authorisation referred to in paragraphs 2 and 3 above may be withdrawn at any time in the best interests of the person concerned.

Article 7 – Protection of persons who have a mental disorder

Subject to protective conditions prescribed by law, including supervisory, control and appeal procedures, a person who has a mental disorder of a serious nature may be subjected, without his or her consent, to an intervention aimed at treating his or her mental disorder only where, without such treatment, serious harm is likely to result to his or her health.

Article 8 – Emergency situation

When because of an emergency situation the appropriate consent cannot be obtained, any medically necessary intervention may be carried out immediately for the benefit of the health of the individual concerned.

Article 9 – Previously expressed wishes

The previously expressed wishes relating to a medical intervention by a patient who is not, at the time of the intervention, in a state to express his or her wishes shall be taken into account.

Chapter III – Private life and right to information

Article 10 – Private life and right to information

1 Everyone has the right to respect for private life in relation to information about his or her health.
2 Everyone is entitled to know any information collected about his or her health. However, the wishes of individuals not to be so informed shall be observed.
3 In exceptional cases, restrictions may be placed by law on the exercise of the rights contained in paragraph 2 in the interests of the patient.

Chapter IV – Human genome

Article 11 – Non-discrimination

Any form of discrimination against a person on grounds of his or her genetic heritage is prohibited.

Article 12 – Predictive genetic tests

Tests which are predictive of genetic diseases or which serve either to identify the subject as a carrier of a gene responsible for a disease or to detect a genetic predisposition or susceptibility to a disease may be performed only for health purposes or for scientific research linked to health purposes, and subject to appropriate genetic counselling.

Article 13 – Interventions on the human genome

An intervention seeking to modify the human genome may only be undertaken for preventive, diagnostic or therapeutic purposes and only if its aim is not to introduce any modification in the genome of any descendants.

Article 14 – Non-selection of sex

The use of techniques of medically assisted procreation shall not be allowed for the purpose of choosing a future child's sex, except where serious hereditary sex-related disease is to be avoided.

Chapter V – Scientific research

Article 15 – General rule

Scientific research in the field of biology and medicine shall be carried out freely, subject to the provisions of this Convention and the other legal provisions ensuring the protection of the human being.

Article 16 – Protection of persons undergoing research

Research on a person may only be undertaken if all the following conditions are met:

- i there is no alternative of comparable effectiveness to research on humans;
- ii the risks which may be incurred by that person are not disproportionate to the potential benefits of the research;
- iii the research project has been approved by the competent body after independent examination of its scientific merit, including assessment of the importance of the aim of the research, and multidisciplinary review of its ethical acceptability;
- iv the persons undergoing research have been informed of their rights and the safeguards prescribed by law for their protection;

v the necessary consent as provided for under Article 5 has been given expressly, specifically and is documented. Such consent may be freely withdrawn at any time.

Article 17 – Protection of persons not able to consent to research

1 Research on a person without the capacity to consent as stipulated in Article 5 may be undertaken only if all the following conditions are met:
   i the conditions laid down in Article 16, sub-paragraphs i to iv, are fulfilled;
   ii the results of the research have the potential to produce real and direct benefit to his or her health;
   iii research of comparable effectiveness cannot be carried out on individuals capable of giving consent;
   iv the necessary authorisation provided for under Article 6 has been given specifically and in writing; and
   v the person concerned does not object.

2 Exceptionally and under the protective conditions prescribed by law, where the research has not the potential to produce results of direct benefit to the health of the person concerned, such research may be authorised subject to the conditions laid down in paragraph 1, sub-paragraphs i, iii, iv and v above, and to the following additional conditions:
   i the research has the aim of contributing, through significant improvement in the scientific understanding of the individual's condition, disease or disorder, to the ultimate attainment of results capable of conferring benefit to the person concerned or to other persons in the same age category or afflicted with the same disease or disorder or having the same condition;
   ii the research entails only minimal risk and minimal burden for the individual concerned.

Article 18 – Research on embryos in vitro

1 Where the law allows research on embryos *in vitro*, it shall ensure adequate protection of the embryo.
2 The creation of human embryos for research purposes is prohibited.

Chapter VI – Organ and tissue removal from living donors for transplantation purposes

Article 19 – General rule

1 Removal of organs or tissue from a living person for transplantation purposes may be carried out solely for the therapeutic benefit of the recipient and where there is no suitable organ or tissue available from a deceased person and no other alternative therapeutic method of comparable effectiveness.

2 The necessary consent as provided for under Article 5 must have been given expressly and specifically either in written form or before an official body.

Article 20 – Protection of persons not able to consent to organ removal

1 No organ or tissue removal may be carried out on a person who does not have the capacity to consent under Article 5.

2 Exceptionally and under the protective conditions prescribed by law, the removal of regenerative tissue from a person who does not have the capacity to consent may be authorised provided the following conditions are met:
- i there is no compatible donor available who has the capacity to consent;
- ii the recipient is a brother or sister of the donor;
- iii the donation must have the potential to be life-saving for the recipient;
- iv the authorisation provided for under paragraphs 2 and 3 of Article 6 has been given specifically and in writing, in accordance with the law and with the approval of the competent body;
- v the potential donor concerned does not object.

Chapter VII – Prohibition of financial gain and disposal of a part of the human body

Article 21 – Prohibition of financial gain

The human body and its parts shall not, as such, give rise to financial gain.

Article 22 – Disposal of a removed part of the human body

When in the course of an intervention any part of a human body is removed, it may be stored and used for a purpose other than that for which it was removed, only if this is done in conformity with appropriate information and consent procedures.

Chapter VIII – Infringements of the provisions of the Convention

Article 23 – Infringement of the rights or principles

The Parties shall provide appropriate judicial protection to prevent or to put a stop to an unlawful infringement of the rights and principles set forth in this Convention at short notice.

Article 24 – Compensation for undue damage

The person who has suffered undue damage resulting from an intervention is entitled to fair compensation according to the conditions and procedures prescribed by law.

Article 25 – Sanctions

Parties shall provide for appropriate sanctions to be applied in the event of infringement of the provisions contained in this Convention.

Chapter IX – Relation between this Convention and other provisions

Article 26 – Restrictions on the exercise of the rights

1 No restrictions shall be placed on the exercise of the rights and protective provisions contained in this Convention other than such as are prescribed by law and are necessary in a democratic society in the interest of public safety, for the prevention of crime, for the protection of public health or for the protection of the rights and freedoms of others.
2 The restrictions contemplated in the preceding paragraph may not be placed on Articles 11, 13, 14, 16, 17, 19, 20 and 21.

Article 27 – Wider protection

None of the provisions of this Convention shall be interpreted as limiting or otherwise affecting the possibility for a Party to grant a wider measure of protection with regard to the application of biology and medicine than is stipulated in this Convention.

Chapter X – Public debate

Article 28 – Public debate

Parties to this Convention shall see to it that the fundamental questions raised by the developments of biology and medicine are the subject of appropriate public discussion in the light, in particular, of relevant medical, social, economic, ethical and legal implications, and that their possible application is made the subject of appropriate consultation.

Chapter XI – Interpretation and follow-up of the Convention

Article 29 – Interpretation of the Convention

The European Court of Human Rights may give, without direct reference to any specific proceedings pending in a court, advisory opinions on legal questions concerning the interpretation of the present Convention at the request of:

- the Government of a Party, after having informed the other Parties;
- the Committee set up by Article 32, with membership restricted to the Representatives of the Parties to this Convention, by a decision adopted by a two-thirds majority of votes cast.

Article 30 – Reports on the application of the Convention

On receipt of a request from the Secretary General of the Council of Europe any Party shall furnish an explanation of the manner in which its internal law ensures the effective implementation of any of the provisions of the Convention.

Chapter XII – Protocols

Article 31 – Protocols

Protocols may be concluded in pursuance of Article 32, with a view to developing, in specific fields, the principles contained in this Convention.

The Protocols shall be open for signature by Signatories of the Convention. They shall be subject to ratification, acceptance or approval. A Signatory may not ratify, accept or approve Protocols without previously or simultaneously ratifying accepting or approving the Convention.

Chapter XIII – Amendments to the Convention

Article 32 – Amendments to the Convention

1 The tasks assigned to 'the Committee' in the present article and in Article 29 shall be carried out by the Steering Committee on Bioethics (CDBI), or by any other committee designated to do so by the Committee of Ministers.

2 Without prejudice to the specific provisions of Article 29, each member State of the Council of Europe, as well as each Party to the present Convention which is not a member of the Council of Europe, may be represented and have one vote in the Committee when the Committee carries out the tasks assigned to it by the present Convention.
3 Any State referred to in Article 33 or invited to accede to the Convention in accordance with the provisions of Article 34 which is not Party to this Convention may be represented on the Committee by an observer. If the European Community is not a Party it may be represented on the Committee by an observer.
4 In order to monitor scientific developments, the present Convention shall be examined within the Committee no later than five years from its entry into force and thereafter at such intervals as the Committee may determine.
5 Any proposal for an amendment to this Convention, and any proposal for a Protocol or for an amendment to a Protocol, presented by a Party, the Committee or the Committee of Ministers shall be communicated to the Secretary General of the Council of Europe and forwarded by him to the member States of the Council of Europe, to the European Community, to any Signatory, to any Party, to any State invited to sign this Convention in accordance with the provisions of Article 33 and to any State invited to accede to it in accordance with the provisions of Article 34.
6 The Committee shall examine the proposal not earlier than two months after it has been forwarded by the Secretary General in accordance with paragraph 5. The Committee shall submit the text adopted by a two-thirds majority of the votes cast to the Committee of Ministers for approval. After its approval, this text shall be forwarded to the Parties for ratification, acceptance or approval.
7 Any amendment shall enter into force, in respect of those Parties which have accepted it, on the first day of the month following the expiration of a period of one month after the date on which five Parties, including at least four member States of the Council of Europe, have informed the Secretary General that they have accepted it.

In respect of any Party which subsequently accepts it, the amendment shall enter into force on the first day of the month following the expiration of a period of one month after the date on which that Party has informed the Secretary General of its acceptance.

Chapter XIV – Final clauses

Article 33 – Signature, ratification and entry into force

1 This Convention shall be open for signature by the member States of the Council of Europe, the non-member States which have participated in its elaboration and by the European Community.

2 This Convention is subject to ratification, acceptance or approval. Instruments of ratification, acceptance or approval shall be deposited with the Secretary General of the Council of Europe.

3 This Convention shall enter into force on the first day of the month following the expiration of a period of three months after the date on which five States, including at least four member States of the Council of Europe, have expressed their consent to be bound by the Convention in accordance with the provisions of paragraph 2 of the present article.

4 In respect of any Signatory which subsequently expresses its consent to be bound by it, the Convention shall enter into force on the first day of the month following the expiration of a period of three months after the date of the deposit of its instrument of ratification, acceptance or approval.

Article 34 – Non-member States

1 After the entry into force of this Convention, the Committee of Ministers of the Council of Europe may, after consultation of the Parties, invite any non-member State of the Council of Europe to accede to this Convention by a decision taken by the majority provided for in Article 20, paragraph d, of the Statute of the Council of Europe, and by the unanimous vote of the representatives of the Contracting States entitled to sit on the Committee of Ministers.

2 In respect of any acceding State, the Convention shall enter into force on the first day of the month following

the expiration of a period of three months after the date of deposit of the instrument of accession with the Secretary General of the Council of Europe.

Article 35 – Territories

1 Any Signatory may, at the time of signature or when depositing its instrument of ratification, acceptance or approval, specify the territory or territories to which this Convention shall apply. Any other State may formulate the same declaration when depositing its instrument of accession.

2 Any Party may, at any later date, by a declaration addressed to the Secretary General of the Council of Europe, extend the application of this Convention to any other territory specified in the declaration and for whose international relations it is responsible or on whose behalf it is authorised to give undertakings. In respect of such territory the Convention shall enter into force on the first day of the month following the expiration of a period of three months after the date of receipt of such declaration by the Secretary General.

3 Any declaration made under the two preceding paragraphs may, in respect of any territory specified in such declaration, be withdrawn by a notification addressed to the Secretary General. The withdrawal shall become effective on the first day of the month following the expiration of a period of three months after the date of receipt of such notification by the Secretary General.

Article 36 – Reservations

1 Any State and the European Community may, when signing this Convention or when depositing the instrument of ratification, acceptance, approval or accession, make a reservation in respect of any particular provision of the Convention to the extent that any law then in force in its territory is not in conformity with the provision. Reservations of a general character shall not be permitted under this article.

2 Any reservation made under this article shall contain a brief statement of the relevant law.

3 Any Party which extends the application of this Convention to a territory mentioned in the declaration referred to in Article 35, paragraph 2, may, in respect of the territory concerned, make a reservation in accordance with the provisions of the preceding paragraphs.

4 Any Party which has made the reservation mentioned in this article may withdraw it by means of a declaration addressed to the Secretary General of the Council of Europe. The withdrawal shall become effective on the first day of the month following the expiration of a period of one month after the date of its receipt by the Secretary General.

Article 37 – Denunciation

1 Any Party may at any time denounce this Convention by means of a notification addressed to the Secretary General of the Council of Europe.

2 Such denunciation shall become effective on the first day of the month following the expiration of a period of three months after the date of receipt of the notification by the Secretary General.

Article 38 – Notifications

The Secretary General of the Council of Europe shall notify the member States of the Council, the European Community, any Signatory, any Party and any other State which has been invited to accede to this Convention of:

a any signature;
b the deposit of any instrument of ratification, acceptance, approval or accession;
c any date of entry into force of this Convention in accordance with Articles 33 or 34;
d any amendment or Protocol adopted in accordance with Article 32, and the date on which such an amendment or Protocol enters into force;
e any declaration made under the provisions of Article 35;
f any reservation and withdrawal of reservation made in pursuance of the provisions of Article 36;
g any other act, notification or communication relating to this Convention.

In witness whereof the undersigned, being duly authorised thereto, have signed this Convention.

Done at Oviedo (Asturias), this 4th day of April 1997, in English and French, both texts being equally authentic, in a single copy which shall be deposited in the archives of the Council of Europe. The Secretary General of the Council of

Europe shall transmit certified copies to each member State of the Council of Europe, to the European Community, to the non-member States which have participated in the elaboration of this Convention, and to any State invited to accede to this Convention.

(3) World Medical Association Declaration of Helsinki

Ethical Principles for Medical Research Involving Human Subjects

Adopted by the 18th WMA General Assembly Helsinki, Finland, June 1964 and amended by the
29th WMA General Assembly, Tokyo, Japan, October 1975
35th WMA General Assembly, Venice, Italy, October 1983
41st WMA General Assembly, Hong Kong, September 1989
48th WMA General Assembly, Somerset West, Republic of South Africa, October 1996
52nd WMA General Assembly, Edinburgh, Scotland, October 2000

A. INTRODUCTION

1. The World Medical Association has developed the Declaration of Helsinki as a statement of ethical principles to provide guidance to physicians and other participants in medical research involving human subjects. Medical research involving human subjects includes research on identifiable human material or identifiable data.
2. It is the duty of the physician to promote and safeguard the health of the people. The physician's knowledge and conscience are dedicated to the fulfillment of this duty.
3. The Declaration of Geneva of the World Medical Association binds the physician with the words, 'The health of my patient will be my first consideration', and the International Code of Medical Ethics declares that, 'A physician shall act only in the patient's interest when providing medical care which might have the effect of weakening the physical and mental condition of the patient'.

4. Medical progress is based on research which ultimately must rest in part on experimentation involving human subjects.
5. In medical research on human subjects, considerations related to the well-being of the human subject should take precedence over the interests of science and society.
6. The primary purpose of medical research involving human subjects is to improve prophylactic, diagnostic and therapeutic procedures and the understanding of the aetiology and pathogenesis of disease. Even the best proven prophylactic, diagnostic, and therapeutic methods must continuously be challenged through research for their effectiveness, efficiency, accessibility and quality.
7. In current medical practice and in medical research, most prophylactic, diagnostic and therapeutic procedures involve risks and burdens.
8. Medical research is subject to ethical standards that promote respect for all human beings and protect their health and rights. Some research populations are vulnerable and need special protection. The particular needs of the economically and medically disadvantaged must be recognized. Special attention is also required for those who cannot give or refuse consent for themselves, for those who may be subject to giving consent under duress, for those who will not benefit personally from the research and for those for whom the research is combined with care.
9. Research Investigators should be aware of the ethical, legal and regulatory requirements for research on human subjects in their own countries as well as applicable international requirements. No national ethical, legal or regulatory requirement should be allowed to reduce or eliminate any of the protections for human subjects set forth in this Declaration.

B. BASIC PRINCIPLES FOR ALL MEDICAL RESEARCH

10. It is the duty of the physician in medical research to protect the life, health, privacy, and dignity of the human subject.
11. Medical research involving human subjects must conform to generally accepted scientific principles, be based on a

thorough knowledge of the scientific literature, other relevant sources of information, and on adequate laboratory and, where appropriate, animal experimentation.

12. Appropriate caution must be exercised in the conduct of research which may affect the environment, and the welfare of animals used for research must be respected.
13. The design and performance of each experimental procedure involving human subjects should be clearly formulated in an experimental protocol. This protocol should be submitted for consideration, comment, guidance, and where appropriate, approval to a specially appointed ethical review committee, which must be independent of the investigator, the sponsor or any other kind of undue influence. This independent committee should be in conformity with the laws and regulations of the country in which the research experiment is performed. The committee has the right to monitor ongoing trials. The researcher has the obligation to provide monitoring information to the committee, especially any serious adverse events. The researcher should also submit to the committee, for review, information regarding funding, sponsors, institutional affiliations, other potential conflicts of interest and incentives for subjects.
14. The research protocol should always contain a statement of the ethical considerations involved and should indicate that there is compliance with the principles enunciated in this Declaration.
15. Medical research involving human subjects should be conducted only by scientifically qualified persons and under the supervision of a clinically competent medical person. The responsibility for the human subject must always rest with a medically qualified person and never rest on the subject of the research, even though the subject has given consent.
16. Every medical research project involving human subjects should be preceded by careful assessment of predictable risks and burdens in comparison with foreseeable benefits to the subject or to others. This does not preclude the participation of healthy volunteers in medical research. The design of all studies should be publicly available.

17. Physicians should abstain from engaging in research projects involving human subjects unless they are confident that the risks involved have been adequately assessed and can be satisfactorily managed. Physicians should cease any investigation if the risks are found to outweigh the potential benefits or if there is conclusive proof of positive and beneficial results.
18. Medical research involving human subjects should only be conducted if the importance of the objective outweighs the inherent risks and burdens to the subject. This is especially important when the human subjects are healthy volunteers.
19. Medical research is only justified if there is a reasonable likelihood that the populations in which the research is carried out stand to benefit from the results of the research.
20. The subjects must be volunteers and informed participants in the research project.
21. The right of research subjects to safeguard their integrity must always be respected. Every precaution should be taken to respect the privacy of the subject, the confidentiality of the patient's information and to minimize the impact of the study on the subject's physical and mental integrity and on the personality of the subject.
22. In any research on human beings, each potential subject must be adequately informed of the aims, methods, sources of funding, any possible conflicts of interest, institutional affiliations of the researcher, the anticipated benefits and potential risks of the study and the discomfort it may entail. The subject should be informed of the right to abstain from participation in the study or to withdraw consent to participate at any time without reprisal. After ensuring that the subject has understood the information, the physician should then obtain the subject's freely-given informed consent, preferably in writing. If the consent cannot be obtained in writing, the non-written consent must be formally documented and witnessed.
23. When obtaining informed consent for the research project the physician should be particularly cautious if the

subject is in a dependent relationship with the physician or may consent under duress. In that case the informed consent should be obtained by a well-informed physician who is not engaged in the investigation and who is completely independent of this relationship.

24. For a research subject who is legally incompetent, physically or mentally incapable of giving consent or is a legally incompetent minor, the investigator must obtain informed consent from the legally authorized representative in accordance with applicable law. These groups should not be included in research unless the research is necessary to promote the health of the population represented and this research cannot instead be performed on legally competent persons.
25. When a subject deemed legally incompetent, such as a minor child, is able to give assent to decisions about participation in research, the investigator must obtain that assent in addition to the consent of the legally authorized representative.
26. Research on individuals from whom it is not possible to obtain consent, including proxy or advance consent, should be done only if the physical/mental condition that prevents obtaining informed consent is a necessary characteristic of the research population. The specific reasons for involving research subjects with a condition that renders them unable to give informed consent should be stated in the experimental protocol for consideration and approval of the review committee. The protocol should state that consent to remain in the research should be obtained as soon as possible from the individual or a legally authorized surrogate.
27. Both authors and publishers have ethical obligations. In publication of the results of research, the investigators are obliged to preserve the accuracy of the results. Negative as well as positive results should be published or otherwise publicly available. Sources of funding, institutional affiliations and any possible conflicts of interest should be declared in the publication. Reports of experimentation not in accordance with the principles laid down in this Declaration should not be accepted for publication.

C. ADDITIONAL PRINCIPLES FOR MEDICAL RESEARCH COMBINED WITH MEDICAL CARE

28. The physician may combine medical research with medical care, only to the extent that the research is justified by its potential prophylactic, diagnostic or therapeutic value. When medical research is combined with medical care, additional standards apply to protect the patients who are research subjects.
29. The benefits, risks, burdens and effectiveness of a new method should be tested against those of the best current prophylactic, diagnostic, and therapeutic methods. This does not exclude the use of placebo, or no treatment, in studies where no proven prophylactic, diagnostic or therapeutic method exists.
30. At the conclusion of the study, every patient entered into the study should be assured of access to the best proven prophylactic, diagnostic and therapeutic methods identified by the study.
31. The physician should fully inform the patient which aspects of the care are related to the research. The refusal of a patient to participate in a study must never interfere with the patient-physician relationship.

    In the treatment of a patient, where proven prophylactic, diagnostic and therapeutic methods do not exist or have been ineffective, the physician, with informed consent from the patient, must be free to use unproven or new prophylactic, diagnostic and therapeutic measures, if in the physician's judgement it offers hope of saving life, re-establishing health or alleviating suffering. Where possible, these measures should be made the object of research, designed to evaluate their safety and efficacy. In all cases, new information should be recorded and, where appropriate, published. The other relevant guidelines of this Declaration should be followed.

List of participants

Research ethics workshop, 14–15 July 2000, Tuebingen, Germany

Richard Ashcroft, Imperial College, London, United Kingdom

Ali H. Bardy, National Agency for Medicines, Helsinki, Finland

Jürgen Boomgaarden, University of Tuebingen, Germany

Panagiota Dalla-Vorgia, University of Athens, Greece

Donna Dickenson, University of Birmingham, United Kingdom

Salla Lötjönen, Secretary General, National Research Ethics Council of Finland, Helsinki

Pekka Louhiala, University of Helsinki, Finland

Giovanni Maio, Zentrum für Ethik und Recht in der Medizin, Freiburg, Germany

Georg Marckmann, University of Tuebingen, Germany

Dietrich Rössler, University of Tuebingen, Germany

Paul Wainwright, University of Wales Swansea, United Kingdom

Heather Widdows, University of Birmingham, United Kingdom

Urban Wiesing, University of Tuebingen, Germany

Research ethics workshop, 29–30 September 2000, Hämeenlinna, Finland

Richard Ashcroft, Imperial College, London, United Kingdom

Ali H. Bardy, National Agency for Medicines, Helsinki, Finland

Jürgen Boomgaarden, University of Tuebingen, Germany

Panagiota Dalla-Vorgia, University of Athens, Greece

Donna Dickenson, University of Birmingham, United Kingdom

Melanie Jones, University of Wales Swansea, United Kingdom

Salla Lötjönen, Secretary General, National Research Ethics Council of Finland, Helsinki

Pekka Louhiala, University of Helsinki, Finland

Giovanni Maio, Zentrum für Ethik und Recht in der Medizin, Freiburg, Germany

Juan Viñas-Salas, Institut Borja de Bioetica, Barcelona, Spain

Paul Wainwright, University of Wales Swansea, United Kingdom

Heather Widdows, University of Birmingham, United Kingdom

Urban Wiesing, University of Tuebingen, Germany

User Workshop 'Medical research ethics', 9 June 2001, Tuebingen, Germany

Jürgen Boomgaarden, University of Tuebingen, Germany

Christina Dalla, University of Athens, Greece

Donna Dickenson, University of Birmingham, United Kingdom

Bram Jacobs, University of Maastricht, The Netherlands

Willem Koch, University of Maastricht, The Netherlands

Thieu Lih Ngo, Imperial College, London, United Kingdom

Pekka Louhiala, University of Helsinki, Finland

Nina Moeller, Lancaster University, United Kingdom

Martin Pedersen, Lancaster University, United Kingdom

Neesha Rockwood, Imperial College, London, United Kingdom

Samuli Saarni, University of Helsinki, Finland

Esther van Swieten, University of Maastricht, The Netherlands

Roope Tikkanen, University of Helsinki, Finland

Suoma Toivanen, University of Helsinki, Finland

Saskia Tromp, University of Maastricht, The Netherlands

Elena Tsourdi, University of Athens, Greece

Heather Widdows, University of Birmingham, United Kingdom

Urban Wiesing, University of Tuebingen, Germany

List of critical readers

Inez de Beaufort, Erasmus Universiteit Rotterdam, The Netherlands

Nikola Biller-Andorno, Institut für Ethik und Geschichte der Medizin, Göttingen, Germany

Lucy Frith, University of Liverpool, United Kingdom

Ritva Halila, Valtioneuvosto, Finland

Tony Hope, Institute of Health Sciences, Oxford, United Kingdom

Sakari Karajalainen, Academy of Finland, Helsinki

Claus-Dieter Middel, Institut für Theorie und Geschichte der Medizin, Münster, Germany

Massimo Reichlin, Facoltà di Psicologia, Milano, Italy

Giuseppe Tavormina, Studio Medico di Psichiatria, Provaglio d'Iseo, Italy

Index

General words/phrases

Names: